100 facts

Mummies

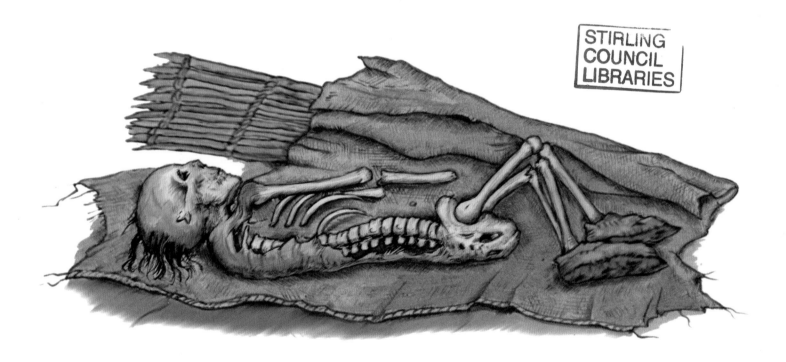

John Malam

Consultant: Fiona MacDonald

J393.3

First published as hardback in 2007 by Miles Kelly Publishing Ltd
Bardfield Centre, Great Bardfield, Essex, CM7 4SL

This edition published 2009

2 4 6 8 10 9 7 5 3 1

Editorial Director: Belinda Gallagher
Art Director: Jo Brewer
Editorial Assistant: Carly Blake
Volume Designer: Sally Lace
Image Manager: Lorraine King
Indexer: Hilary Bird
Production Manager: Elizabeth Brunwin
Reprographics: Anthony Cambray, Liberty Newton, Ian Paulyn
Archive Manager: Jennifer Hunt
Editions Manager: Bethan Ellish
Editions Assistant: Toby Tippen

ISBN 978-1-84810-106-7

Printed in China

British Library Cataloguing-in-Publication Data
A catalogue record for this book is available from the British Library

ACKNOWLEDGEMENTS

The publishers would like to thank the following artists who have contributed to this book:
Jim Eldridge, Mike Foster, Colin Livingstone, Patricia Ludlow, Carlo Pauletto, Mike White
All other artworks are from the Miles Kelly Artwork Bank

The publishers would like to thank the following sources for the use of their photographs:
Cover Iconotec/Alamy; Page 12 Christophe Boisvieux/Corbis; 13 (t) Photolibrary Group LTD;
14 Topham Picturepoint TopFoto.co.uk; 16 (t/r) The British Museum/HIP/TopFoto.co.uk;
28 TopFoto.co.uk; 29 (t) Topham Picturepoint TopFoto.co.uk;
32 (t) Topham Picturepoint TopFoto.co.uk; 36 (b) Werner Forman Archive/The Greenland Museum;
38 (t) Topham Picturepoint TopFoto.co.uk; 38 (b) Charles Walker/TopFoto.co.uk;
39 (c) Fortean/Trottmann/TopFoto.co.uk; 40 (b) Remigiusz Sikora/epa/Corbis;
41 (t) Charles Walker/TopFoto.co.uk; 41 (b) Roger-Viollet/TopFoto.co.uk; 42 (b) TopFoto.co.uk;
43 (c) John Malam; 43 (b) TopFoto/Fotean/TopFoto.co.uk; 44 Topham Picturepoint TopFoto.co.uk;
45 (t) Topham Picturepoint TopFoto.co.uk; 45 (c) TopFoto/HIP/TopFoto.co.uk;
46 (c) RIA Novosti/TopFoto.co.uk; 47 (b) Topham Picturepoint TopFoto.co.uk

All other photographs are from:
Corel, digitalSTOCK, digitalvision, iStockphoto.com, John Foxx,
PhotoAlto, PhotoDisc, PhotoEssentials, PhotoPro, Stockbyte

Made with paper from a sustainable forest

www.mileskelly.net
info@mileskelly.net

www.factsforprojects.com

100 facts

Mummies

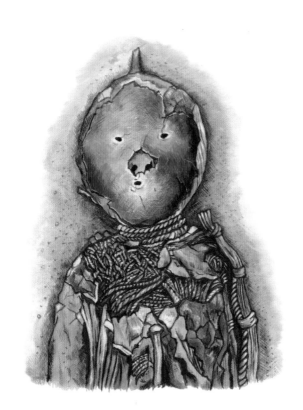

Contents

What is a mummy?

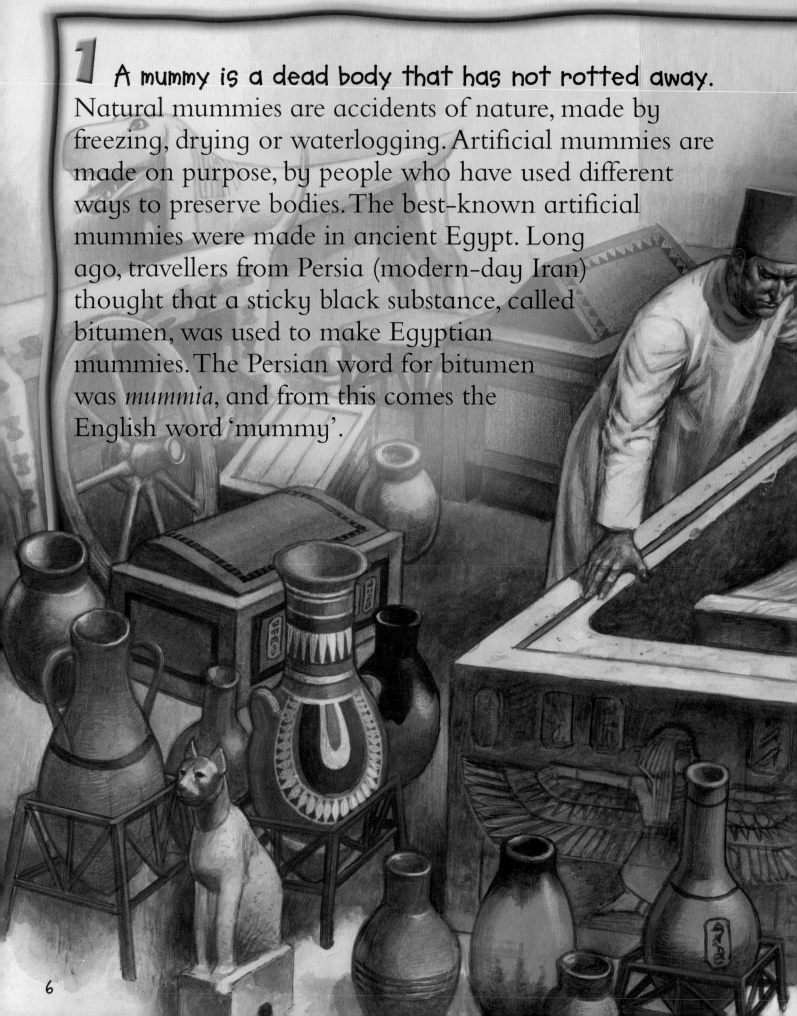

1 **A mummy is a dead body that has not rotted away.** Natural mummies are accidents of nature, made by freezing, drying or waterlogging. Artificial mummies are made on purpose, by people who have used different ways to preserve bodies. The best-known artificial mummies were made in ancient Egypt. Long ago, travellers from Persia (modern-day Iran) thought that a sticky black substance, called bitumen, was used to make Egyptian mummies. The Persian word for bitumen was *mummia*, and from this comes the English word 'mummy'.

▲ The 3300-year-old mummy of Egyptian pharaoh Tutankhamun was discovered in 1922 by Howard Carter. This is a good example of an artificial mummy.

The first mummies

2 The first artificial mummies were made 7000 years ago by the Chinchorro people of South America. These people are named after a place in Chile. Here, scientists discovered traces of the way the Chinchorro lived. They were a fishing people who lived in small groups along the coast of the Pacific Ocean.

QUIZ

1. Where did the Chinchorro people live?
2. What was put on a mummy to make a body shape?
3. For how many years did the Chinchorro make mummies?
4. When were the first mummies discovered?

Answers:
1. Chile in South America
2. White mud 3. 3000 years 4. 1917

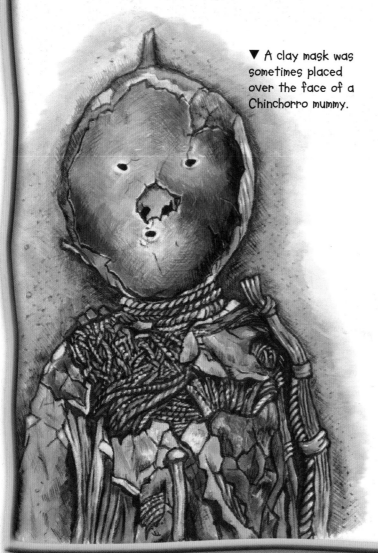

▼ A clay mask was sometimes placed over the face of a Chinchorro mummy.

3 It is thought that the Chinchorro made mummies because they believed in life after death. They tried to make a mummy look as lifelike as possible, which shows they did not want the person's body to rot away. Perhaps they thought the dead could live again if their bodies were preserved.

4 To make a mummy, the Chinchorro first removed all of a dead person's insides. The skin and flesh were then taken off the bones, which were left to dry. Then sticks were tied to the arm, leg and spine bones to hold them together. White mud was spread over the skeleton to build a body shape. The face skin was put back in place, and patches of skin were added to the body. When the mud was dry, it was painted black or red.

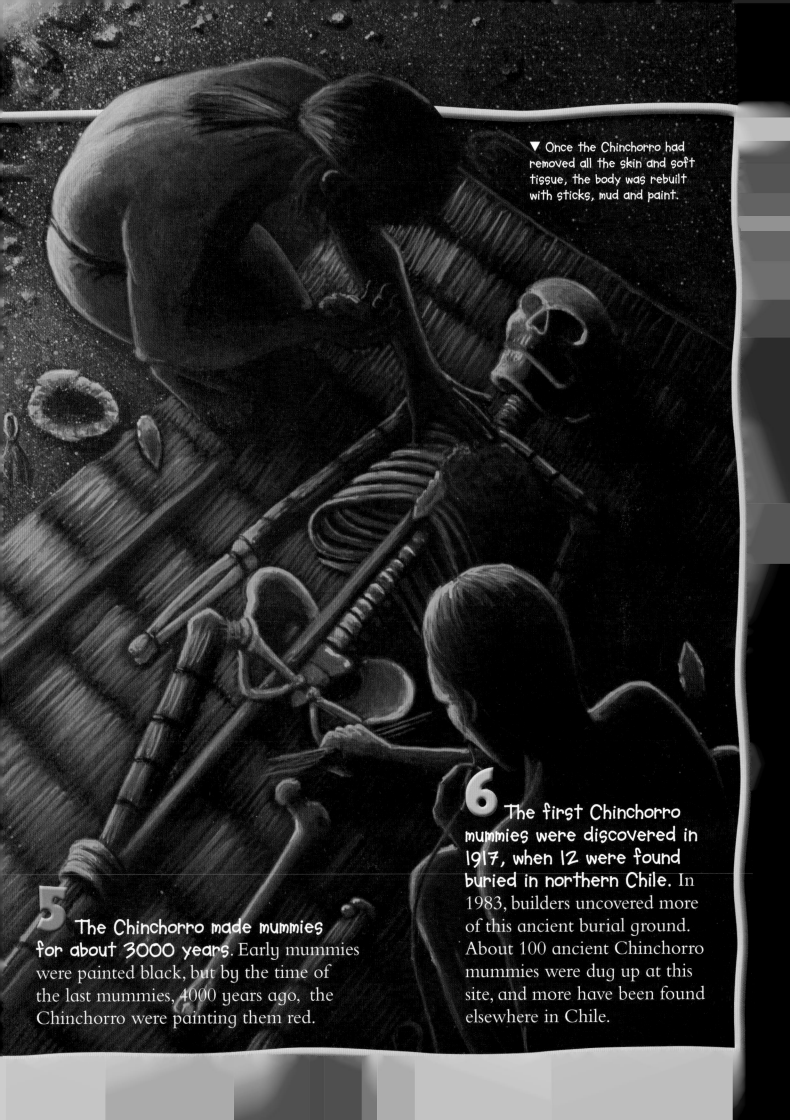

▼ Once the Chinchorro had removed all the skin and soft tissue, the body was rebuilt with sticks, mud and paint.

5 The Chinchorro made mummies for about 3000 years. Early mummies were painted black, but by the time of the last mummies, 4000 years ago, the Chinchorro were painting them red.

6 The first Chinchorro mummies were discovered in 1917, when 12 were found buried in northern Chile. In 1983, builders uncovered more of this ancient burial ground. About 100 ancient Chinchorro mummies were dug up at this site, and more have been found elsewhere in Chile.

Iceman of Europe

7 **Europe's oldest human mummy is known as the Iceman.** He died about 5300 years ago, at the end of the Stone Age. His mummy was discovered by hikers in northern Italy in 1991. They found it lying face down in an icy glacier.

8 **The Iceman mummy was found high up in the mountains, where it is very cold.** At first, people thought that he was a shepherd, or a hunter on the search for food – or even a traveller on a journey. Then in 2001, an arrowhead was found in the Iceman's left shoulder. He might have fled into the mountains to escape danger.

9 **When the Iceman was alive, arrows had sharp points made from flint (a type of stone).** It was a flint arrowhead that injured the Iceman, piercing his clothes and entering his left shoulder. This arrow caused a deep wound. The Iceman pulled the long arrow shaft out, but the arrowhead remained inside his body. This injury would have made the Iceman weak, eventually causing him to die.

◄ The Iceman is the oldest complete human mummy ever to be found. He is so well preserved, even his eyes are still visible.

10 **The mummy's clothes were also preserved by the ice.** For the first time, scientists saw how a Stone Age person actually dressed. The Iceman wore leggings and shoes made from leather, a goatskin coat, a bearskin hat and a cape made from woven grass. These would have kept the Iceman warm in the cold climate.

11 **Equipment used by the Iceman was also found with him.** He carried a copper axe, a flint dagger, and a bow and quiver with 14 arrows. He also had a leather pouch filled with dried grass, which he would have used for starting fires. If the Iceman had been a hunter, he would have killed animals, such as the mountain ibex (a type of goat), with his arrows.

12 **Today, the Iceman mummy and his clothes and equipment are kept at a museum in northern Italy.** Visitors are able to peep through a tiny window to see the Iceman, who is kept frozen inside a special room. The mummy must never be allowed to thaw, as this would cause it to rot.

▶ This reconstruction of the Iceman shows how he would have looked on the day he died.

Quiver to hold arrows

Leather pouch

Flint dagger

Copper axe

Shoes stuffed with grass for warmth

I DON'T BELIEVE IT!

At first, the Iceman was thought to be a modern person who had died in a recent accident on the mountain.

Bog bodies

13 Lots of mummies have been found in the peat bogs of northern Europe. Peat is a soily substance that is formed from plants that have fallen into pools of water. The plants sink to the bottom and are slowly turned into peat. If a dead body is placed in a bog, it may be preserved as a mummy. This is because there is little oxygen or bacteria to rot the body.

▶ The face of Tollund Man is so well preserved, he looks as if he is sleeping.

14 Bog bodies, or mummies, are usually found when peat is dug up. One of the best-known bodies was dug up at Tollund, Denmark, in 1950. Tollund Man, as he is known, died 2300 years ago. Around his neck was a leather noose. He was hanged, perhaps as a sacrifice to his gods, and then thrown in the bog. Over the years his face was perfectly preserved, right down to the whiskers on his chin!

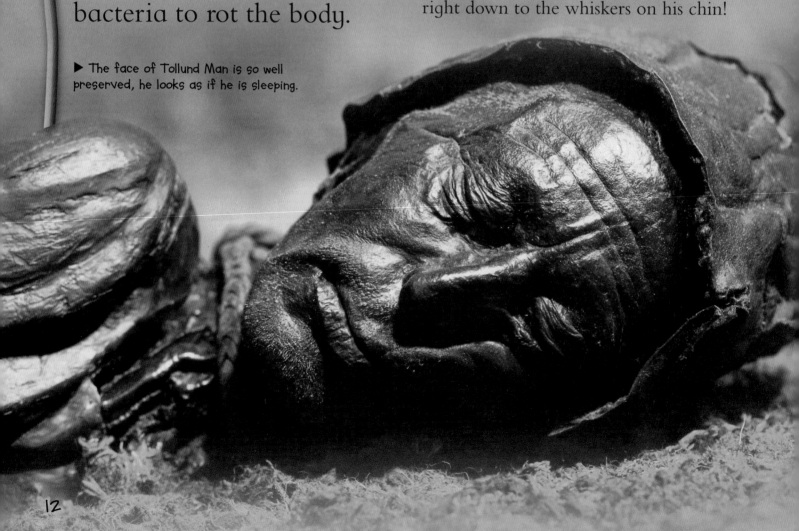

15 Grauballe Man was also found in a peat bog in Denmark. He was discovered by peat workers near the village of Grauballe in 1852. About 2300 years ago, the man's throat was cut and he bled to death. His body was thrown into a bog, where it was preserved until its discovery.

▲ The head of Grauballe Man. Like all bog bodies, his skin has turned brown due to the acids in the bog.

16 Bog bodies have also been discovered in Germany. At Windeby, the body of a teenage girl was found. The girl, who died 1900 years ago, was wearing a blindfold. It seems she was taken to the bog, her eyes were covered, and then she was drowned. A heavy rock and branches were put on top of her body, so it sank to the bottom of the bog.

▶ The mummy of Windeby Girl revealed that some of her hair had been cut off, or shaved, at the time of her death.

17 From the Netherlands comes the bog body of another teenage girl. Known as Yde (*ay-de*) Girl, she was stabbed, strangled and then dumped in a bog around 1900 years ago. A medical artist made a copy of her skull, then covered it with wax to rebuild her face. The model shows scientists how Yde Girl may have looked when she was alive.

Lindow Man

18 A bog body of a man was found in north-west England in 1984. It was discovered by peat cutters at Lindow Moss, Cheshire. The mummy was named 'Lindow Man', but a local newspaper nicknamed it 'Pete Marsh' because a peat bog is a wet, marshy place! Lindow Man is now on display at the British Museum, London.

19 Lindow Man was about 20 years old when he died. His short life came to an end around 1900 years ago. After his death, his body was put in a bog, where it sank without trace until its discovery by the peat cutters.

▼ The body of Lindow Man was squashed flat by the weight of the peat on top of it.

20 Lindow Man did not die peacefully. Before he died, he ate food with poisonous mistletoe in it. It's impossible to say if the poison was put there on purpose, or by accident. The marks on his body tell the story of his last moments alive. Someone hit him hard on the head, a cord was tightened around his neck and he was strangled. Then, to make sure he was dead, his throat was cut.

21 It took four years to find most of Lindow Man's body. The machine used to cut the peat had sliced it into pieces, which were found at different times. His top half, from the waist up, was found in 1984, and four years later his left leg turned up. His right leg is missing, possibly still buried in the peat bog.

▲ In this reconstruction, Lindow Man eats a meal containing burnt bread. This may have been part of a ceremony in which he was sacrificed to the gods.

I DON'T BELIEVE IT!

Visitors to the British Museum have come up with names for Lindow Man, including Sludge Man and Man in the Toilet!

22 In Lindow Man's time, gifts were given to the gods. The greatest gift was a human sacrifice, which is what may have happened to Lindow Man. After eating a meal mixed with mistletoe, he was killed and put in a bog. People thought he was leaving this world and entering the world of the gods.

Mummies of ancient Egypt

23 The most famous mummies were made in ancient Egypt. The Egyptians were skilled embalmers (mummy-makers). Pharaohs (rulers of Egypt) and ordinary people were made into mummies, along with many kinds of animal.

▲ Even pet dogs were mummified in ancient Egypt.

▲ Two people walk through the Field of Reeds, which was the ancient Egyptian name for paradise.

24 Mummies were made because the Egyptians thought that the dead needed their bodies in a new life after death. They believed a person would live forever in paradise, but only if their body was saved. Every Egyptian wanted to travel to paradise after death. This is why they went to such trouble to preserve the bodies of the dead.

25 Ancient Egypt's first mummies were made by nature. When a person died, their body was buried in a pit in the desert sand. The person was buried with objects to use in the next life. Because the sand was hot and dry, the flesh did not rot. Instead, the flesh and skin dried and shrivelled until they were stretched over the bones. The body had been mummified. Egypt's natural mummies date from around 3500 BC.

26 The ancient Egyptians made their first artificial mummies around 3400 BC. The last mummies were made around AD 400. This means the Egyptians were making mummies for 4000 years! They stopped making them because as the Christian religion spread to Egypt, mummy-making came to be seen as a pagan (non-Christian) practice.

◄ This man died 5200 years ago in Egypt. His body slowly dried out in the hot, desert conditions, and became a natural mummy.

27 When an old grave was found, perhaps by robbers who wanted to steal the grave goods, they got a surprise. Instead of digging up a skeleton, they uncovered a dried-up body that still looked like a person! This might have started the ancient Egyptians thinking – could they find a way to preserve bodies themselves?

► Many Egyptian coffins were shaped like a person and beautifully painted and decorated.

Egypt's first mummy

28 The ancient Egyptians told a myth about how the very first mummy was made. The story was about Osiris, who was ruler of Egypt. It explained how Osiris became the first mummy, and because it had happened to him, people wanted to follow his example and be mummified when they died.

29 The story begins with the murder of Osiris. He had a wicked brother called Seth, and one day Seth tricked Osiris into lying inside a box. The box was really a coffin. Seth shut the lid and threw the coffin into the river Nile, and Osiris drowned. Seth killed his brother because he was jealous of him – he felt the people of Egypt did not love him as much as they loved Osiris.

30 Isis was married to Osiris, and she could not bear to be parted from him. She searched throughout Egypt for his body, and when she found it, she brought it home. Isis knew that Seth would be angry if he found out what she had done, and so she hid the dead body of Osiris.

▶ Isis, Anubis and Thoth rebuild the body of Osiris to make the first mummy.

QUIZ

1. Who killed Osiris?
2. Who was the wife of Osiris?
3. How many pieces did Seth cut Osiris into?
4. Which three gods helped Isis?
5. What did Osiris become in the afterlife?

Answers:
1. Seth 2. Isis 3. 14
4. Ra, Anubis, Thoth
5. King of the dead

31 However Seth found out, and he took the body of Osiris from its hiding place. Seth cut Osiris into 14 pieces, which he scattered far and wide across Egypt. At last, he thought, he had finally got rid of Osiris.

32 Seth might have destroyed Osiris, but he could not destroy the love that Isis had for him. Once again, Isis searched for Osiris. She turned herself into a kite (a bird of prey), and flew high above Egypt so she could look down upon the land to see where Seth had hidden the body parts of Osiris. One by one, Isis found the pieces of her husband's body, except for one, which was eaten by a fish.

33 Isis brought the pieces together. She wept at the sight of her husband's body. When Ra, the sun god, saw her tears, he sent the gods Anubis and Thoth to help her. Anubis wrapped the pieces of Osiris' body in cloth. Then Isis, Anubis and Thoth laid them out in the shape of Osiris and wrapped the whole body. The first mummy had been made. Isis kissed the mummy and Osiris was reborn, not to live in this world, but to live forever in the afterlife as king of the dead.

A very messy job

34 Mummies were made in Egypt for almost 4000 years. Mummy-makers experimented with different methods of preserving the dead, some of which worked better than others. The best mummies were made during a time of Egyptian history called the New Kingdom, between 3550 and 3069 years ago.

35 An ancient Greek called Herodotus wrote down one way the Egyptians made mummies. Herodotus visited Egypt in the 400s BC. He was told that it took 70 days to make a mummy – 15 days to cleanse the body, 40 days to dry it out and 15 days to wrap it.

36 Mummy-makers worked in open-air tents. Their simple workshops, which were far from villages and towns, were along the west bank of the river Nile. The tents were left open so that bad smells were carried away on the breeze. They were near the river as water was needed in the mummy-making process.

I DON'T BELIEVE IT!

In the 1800s, Egyptian cat mummies were shipped to England where they were crushed up to make fertilizer!

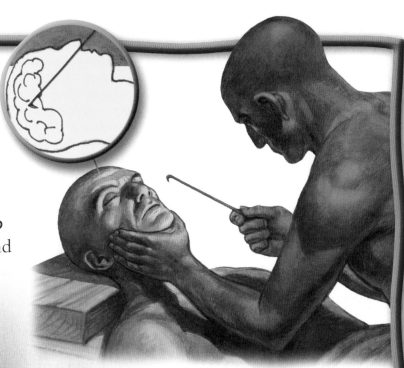

▶ To remove the brain, a metal hook was pushed up through the left nostril. It was then used to pull the brain out through the nose.

37 Mummy–making skills were handed down from one generation to the next. It was a job for men only, and it was a father's duty to train his son. A boy learned by watching his father at work. If his father worked as a slitter – the man who made the first cut in the body – his son also became a slitter.

38 The first 15 days of making a mummy involved cleaning the body. In the Place of Purification tent, the body was washed with salty water. It was then taken to the House of Beauty tent. Here, the brain was removed and thrown away. Then a slit was made in the left side of the body and the liver, lungs, intestines and stomach were taken out and kept.

39 The heart was left inside the body. The Egyptians thought the heart was the centre of intelligence. They believed it was needed to guide the person in the next life. If the heart was removed by mistake, it was put back inside. The kidneys were also left inside the body.

◀ A dead body was carefully washed with salty water before its organs were removed.

Drying the body

40 After the insides had been taken out, the body was dried. Mummy-makers used a special salt called natron to do the drying. The salt was a powdery-white mixture and was found along the edges of lakes in the north of Egypt. The natron was put into baskets, then taken to the mummy-makers.

43 The liver, lungs, intestines and stomach were also dried. Each of these organs was placed in a separate pottery bowl, and natron was piled on top. Just like the body, these organs were also left for 40 days, during which time the natron dried them out.

Bags of natron

Sawdust

Dried grass

41 At the workshop, small linen bags were filled with natron. The bags were packed into the empty body through the slit where the insides had been taken out. As well as the natron, rags, straw, dried grass and sawdust were also stuffed into the body. They helped to give the body its human shape.

▲ Some of the materials used by mummy-makers to stuff the bodies of mummies.

42 Next, the body was placed on its back on a table and covered in a thick layer of natron. No flesh was left exposed. The body was left to dry out under the natron for 40 days.

44 Fisherman first used natron to dry the fish they caught. They realized that natron's salty crystals sucked juices out of dead flesh, leaving it dry. Dried, or salted, fish did not rot. This was why the mummy-makers began to use natron to preserve the dead.

45 During the 40 days of drying, the natron absorbed the body's juices. At the end of this time, the mummy-makers scraped away the natron and removed the materials used to stuff the body. The dried body had lost about three-quarters of its original weight and was shrivelled, hard and blue-black in colour. It hardly looked like a body at all.

▲ The body was covered in natron, a kind of salt, to dry it out. Up to 225 kilograms were needed.

Wrapped from head to toe

46 The next job was to make the body appear lifelike. The body cavity was filled and the skin was rubbed with oil and spices to make it soft and sweet-smelling. Then it was given false eyes and a wig, and make-up was applied. Lastly, tree resin was poured over it. This set into a hard layer to stop mould growing.

47 The dried-out organs were wrapped in linen, then put into containers called canopic jars. The container with the baboon head (the god Hapi) held the lungs, and the stomach was put into the jackal-headed jar (the god Duamutef). The human-headed jar (the god Imseti) protected the liver, and the intestines were placed in the falcon-headed jar (the god Qebehsenuef).

Hapi

Imseti

◄ The four canopic jars represented the sons of the god Horus.

Duamutef

Qebehsenuef

48 The cut on the left side of the body was rarely stitched up. Instead, it was covered with a wax plaque. On the plaque was a design known as the Eye of Horus. The Egyptians believed it had the power to see evil and stop it from entering the body through the cut.

1. Head wrapped

Eye of Horus

49 **In the final part of the process, the body was wrapped.** It took 11 days to do this. The body was wrapped in strips of linen, 6 to 20 centimetres wide. There was a set way of wrapping the body, which always started with the head. Lastly, the body was covered with a sheet of linen, tied with linen bands.

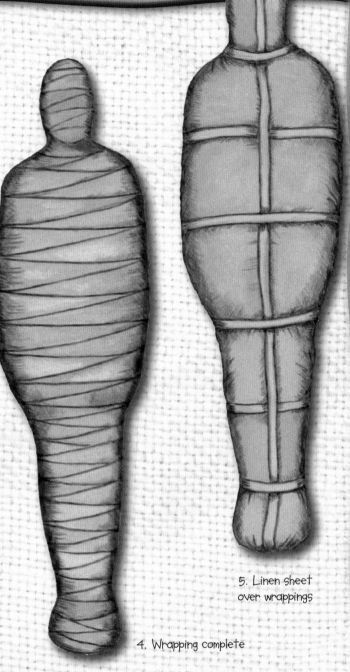

5. Linen sheet over wrappings

4. Wrapping complete

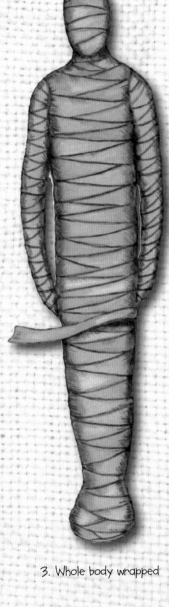

3. Whole body wrapped

▲ There was a five-stage sequence for wrapping the body, which always started with the head.

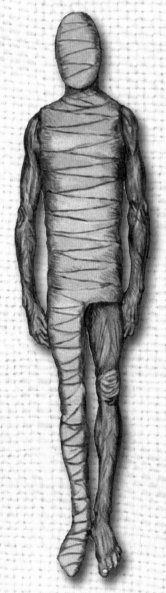

2. Limbs and torso wrapped

50 **During the wrapping, amulets (lucky charms) were placed between the layers of linen.** These protected the person from harm on their journey to the afterlife. Magic spells written on the wrappings were another form of protection. After it was wrapped, resin was poured over the mummy to make it waterproof. Last of all, it was given a face mask.

Tombs and tomb robbers

51 **The body was placed in a wooden coffin.** Simple coffins were made from planks of wood, and expensive ones were shaped like a person. They were decorated with spells. A picture on the inside of the coffin showed the route to the afterlife.

52 **The earliest pharaohs (kings) were buried in pyramid tombs.** The first pyramid was built about 2650 BC, for Pharaoh Djoser. For the next 800 years, all pharaohs were buried in pyramids. However robbers found their way into all of them. Later pharaohs were buried in tombs cut into a rocky valley, known as the Valley of the Kings. Robbers found many of these tombs too, but not all.

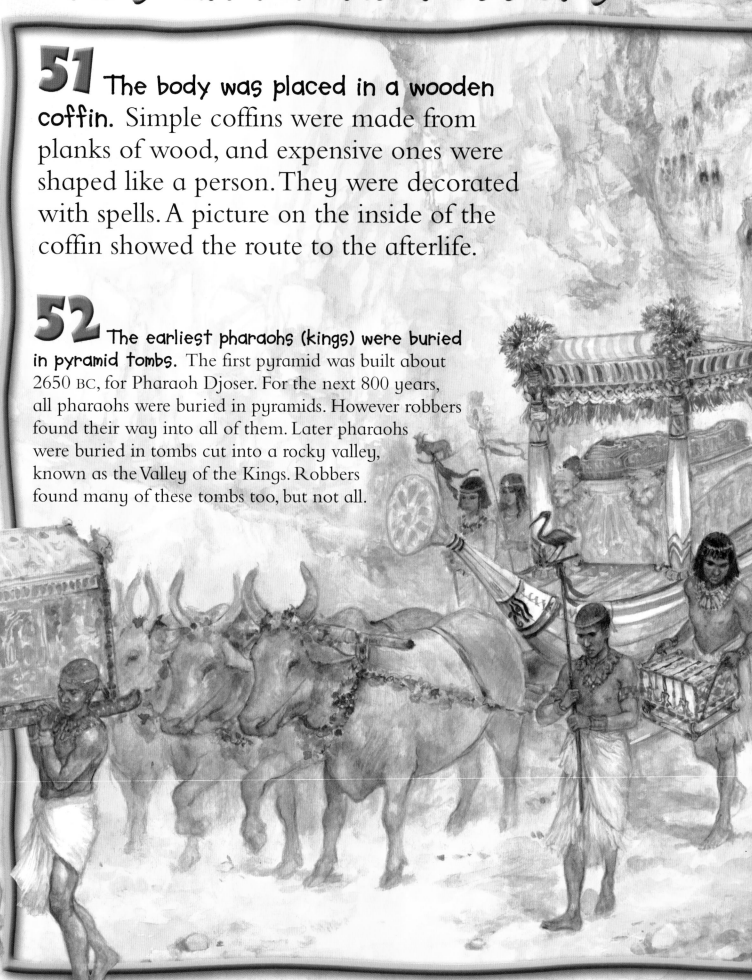

53 On the day of burial, the mummy was lifted out of its coffin and stood upright. A priest used a Y-shaped stone tool to touch the mummy's mouth, eyes, nose and ears. This was the Opening of the Mouth ceremony. It was done so that the person's speech, sight, hearing and smell came back to them for use in the next life.

▲ A priest (right) about to touch a mummy (left) in the Opening of the Mouth ceremony.

54 Mummies were buried with grave goods. These were items for the person to use in the next life. Ordinary people were buried with basic items, such as food and drink. Pharaohs and wealthy people were buried with everything they would need in their next life, such as furniture, clothes, weapons, jewellery and musical instruments.

55 Tombs were tempting places to robbers. They knew what was inside them, and took great risks to break in and steal the goods. Not even a mummy was safe – the tomb robbers smashed coffins open, and cut their way through the layers of linen wrappings to get at the masks, amulets and jewellery. Tomb robbery was a major crime, and if a robber was caught he was put to death.

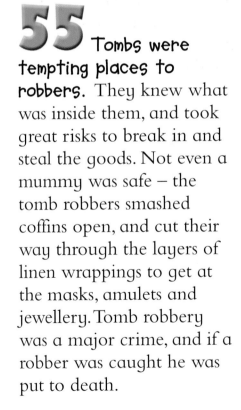

◄ A funeral procession on its way to the Valley of the Kings. Oxen pulled the coffin on a wooden sledge shaped like a boat. This represented the deceased's journey to the next life.

Tutankhamun, the boy-king

56 Tutankhamun is one of Egypt's most famous pharaohs. He became king in 1334 BC when he was eight years old. Because he was too young to carry out the important work of ruling Egypt, two of his ministers took charge. They were Ay, chief minister, and Horemheb, head of the army. They made decisions on Tutankhamun's behalf.

◄ This model of Tutankhamun was buried with him in his tomb.

57 Tutankhamun was pharaoh for about nine years. He died when he was 17 years old. His body was mummified and buried in a tomb cut into the side of a valley. Many pharaohs were laid to rest in this valley, known as the Valley of the Kings. Tutankhamun was buried with valuables for use in the next life.

58 The tombs in the Valley of the Kings were meant to be secret. However robbers found them, and stole the precious items buried there. They found Tutankhamun's tomb, but were caught before they could do much damage. Years later, when the tomb of Rameses VI was being dug, rubble rolled down the valley and blocked the entrance to Tutankhamun's tomb. After that, it was forgotten about.

◀ Tutankhamun's throne. The back is decorated with a picture of the pharaoh, who is seated, and a princess.

59 **In 1922, British archaeologist Howard Carter discovered the tomb of Tutankhamun.** He had spent years searching for it. Other archaeologists thought he was wasting his time. They said all the tombs in the valley had already been found. Carter refused to give up, and in November 1922 he found a stairway that led to the door of a tomb.

60 **Behind the door was a corridor.** At the end of it was a second door, which Carter made a hole in. He peered through the hole, and said he could see 'wonderful things'. It took ten years to remove all the objects from the tomb – jewellery and a gold throne were among the treasures. A gold mask covered the king's head and shoulders. It was made of 10 kilograms of pure gold.

▼ Tutankhamun was buried in three separate coffins that fitted inside each other. This is the middle coffin, which is made of gold and decorated with a gem called lapis lazuli.

Magnificent mummies!

61 The mummy of pharaoh Rameses II was found in 1871. It had been buried in a tomb, but had been moved to prevent robbers finding it. Rameses II had bad teeth, probably caused by eating gritty bread. He was in his eighties when he died and had arthritis, which would have given him painful joints. In 1976 his mummy was sent to France for treatment to stop mould from damaging it.

62 Mummy 1770 is in the Manchester Museum, in the UK. This is a mummy of a teenage girl, whose real name is not known. Her lower legs and feet are missing, and the mummy-makers had given her false ones to make her appear whole. It's a mystery what happened to her, but she might have been bitten by a crocodile, or even a hippo, as she paddled in the river Nile 3000 years ago.

▼ The mummy of Rameses II. Scientific studies have shown that particularly fine linen was used to stuff and bandage the body.

63
A trapped donkey led to the discovery of thousands of mummies! It happened in 1996, when a donkey slipped into a hole at Egypt's Bahariya Oasis. The owner freed it, then climbed down into an underground system of chambers lined with thousands of mummies of ordinary people. The site is called the Valley of the Golden Mummies, as many of the mummies have golden masks over their faces. They are about 2000 years old.

64
Djedmaatesankh – Djed for short – is an Egyptian mummy in the Royal Ontario Museum, Toronto, Canada. She lived around 850 BC, and in 1977 she entered the history books as the first Egyptian mummy to have a whole-body CAT scan (computerized axial tomography). The CAT images revealed that Djed had a serious infection in her jaw, which may have caused her death.

QUIZ

1. What was damaging Rameses II?
2. What is false about Mummy 1770?
3. What did a donkey help to find?
4. Which mummy had the first CAT scan?

Answers:
1. Mould 2. Her legs and feet
3. The Valley of the Golden Mummies
4. Djed

Mummies of Peru

65 Mummies were made in Peru, South America, for hundreds of years. The first were made in the 400s BC, and the last probably in the early 1500s AD. A body was put into a sitting position, with its knees tucked under its chin. Layers of cloth were wrapped around it to make a 'mummy bundle'. The body was preserved by the dry, cold environment.

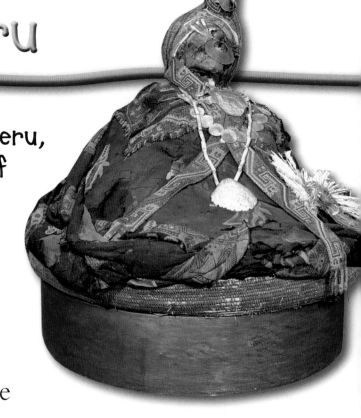

▲ This mummy from Peru is more than 500 years old. It was covered in cloth to make a 'mummy bundle'.

▲ Mummies of emperors were carried through the streets and put on display to the public.

66 In the 1500s, the mummies of Inca emperors were paraded through the streets of Cuzco, Peru. People thought that by doing this the souls of the dead were well-cared for, and this helped them on their journey into the afterlife. People also believed that this practice pleased the gods, who then ensured that living people were healthy and happy.

I DON'T BELIEVE IT!

When Spaniards came to Peru in the 1500s, they destroyed thousands of Inca mummies – they got rid of 1365 in just four years!

67 The Incas sacrificed children to their gods.

They hoped that in return the gods would provide rain for crops, good health and prosperity. The children's bodies were left at the tops of freezing mountains, where they slowly turned into natural mummies.

68 In 1995, the mummy of a teenage Inca girl was found.

She was led to her death 500 years ago, as a sacrifice to the gods. Her body was left 6300 metres up Mount Ampato, Peru, with offerings of cloth, food, gold and silver. The icy conditions preserved her body.

▶ Inca children stand in front of a priest as they prepare to be sacrificed to the gods in a religious ceremony.

Mummies from Asia

69 More than 2500 years ago, the Pazyryk people of Siberia, Russia, buried their leaders in the region's frozen ground. In 1993, a Pazyryk burial mound was dug up, and inside was the frozen mummy of the 'Ice Princess'. She was dressed in clothes made from silk and wool, and she wore a pair of riding boots. When her body thawed from the ice, pictures of deer were found tattooed on her skin.

▲ The Pazyryk people tattooed images of snow leopards, eagles and reindeer onto their bodies. Those found on the 'Ice Princess' may have been a mark of her importance, or rank.

70 Lady Ch'eng is one of the world's best-preserved mummies. She was found in China, and is 2100 years old. Her body had been placed inside a coffin filled with a strange liquid that contained mercury (a silvery liquid metal, also known as quicksilver). The coffin was sealed and placed inside another, and then another. The coffins were buried under a mound of charcoal and clay, and in this watertight, airtight tomb her body was preserved.

◄ This artist's impression shows how Lady Ch'eng may have looked when she was alive more than 2000 years ago.

QUIZ

1. What country did Vu Khac Minh come from?
2. What metal was in Lady Ch'eng's coffin?
3. What was on the skin of the Ice Princess?
4. How old are the Taklamakan mummies?

Answers:
1. Vietnam 2. Mercury
3. Tattoos 4. 3000 years

72 **Vu Khac Minh was a Buddhist monk from Vietnam.** In 1639, when he was near the end of his life, he locked himself in his room. He told his fellow monks to leave him alone for 100 days while he meditated (prayed). When this time was up, the monks found that he had died. His body was perfectly preserved and was put on view for all to see.

71 **Mummies have been found in China's Taklamakan Desert.** It hardly rains here, and the salty sand means that human bodies do not rot. It was a surprise when mummies were found in this remote place. They are about 3000 years old, and look Indo-European, not Chinese. It seems that long ago, a group of tall, light-skinned people settled in the east, where they died and were buried.

◀ Cherchen Man was just one of the many mummies found in the Taklamakan Desert.

35

North American mummies

73 **At 9000 years old, Spirit Cave Man is one of the oldest mummies.** The mummy was found in Spirit Cave, Nevada, USA, in 1940. It was wearing a cloak of animal skins, leather moccasins on its feet, and was wrapped inside mats made of tough grass. The cool, dry air in the cave had dried the body, turning it into a natural mummy.

▲ The mummy of Spirit Cave Man. Although it was discovered in 1940, the mummy's actual age was not determined until 1994.

I DON'T BELIEVE IT!

Hazel Farris, like Elmer McCurdy, was another American outlaw whose mummified body was put on show at funfairs.

75 **A mummy family was found on Greenland in 1972.** The bodies of six Inuit women and two children had been placed on a rocky ledge, in about 1475. The cold conditions had preserved them, slowly freeze-drying their bodies.

74 **The mummy of the North American Iceman no longer exists.** It was found in 1999, in Canada. The Iceman had died in the 1400s, and was preserved in a glacier. Native North Americans claimed that the man was their ancestor, so the mummy was handed to them. It was cremated, and the ashes buried near where the mummy had been found.

▲ An Inuit mummy of a baby boy. He was killed so that he could stay with his mother in the afterlife.

76 Elmer McCurdy was an American outlaw who became a mummy! He was shot dead in 1911 after robbing a train. His body was taken to an undertakers where it was preserved, but no one claimed the body. Eventually, McCurdy's mummy was sold to a fairground. In 1976, a TV programme was being filmed at a ghost ride, and a 'dummy' turned out to be the mummy of Elmer McCurdy! He was finally buried in 1977.

77 The mummies of three British sailors lie in the frozen ground of the Arctic. They are John Torrington, John Hartnell and William Braine, who died in 1845 during a voyage from England to find a sea route across the Arctic Ocean. Their bodies were examined in 1984, and it was discovered that they had suffered from lead poisoning, caused by eating contaminated food. The sailors were reburied, and the Arctic began to freeze their bodies again.

▼ The crew of HMS *Terror* try to dig their ship out of the Arctic ice. The men eventually died, and some of their remains were mummified in the freezing conditions.

Worldwide mummies

78 **Mount Vesuvius is a volcano in southern Italy.** It erupted in AD 79, and the town of Pompeii was buried under a layer of ash and rock. Many people died, mostly by suffocation. As scientists uncovered the town, they found body-shaped areas in the ground. By pouring plaster of Paris into the areas, the shapes of the dead were revealed.

▲ This plaster cast shows a victim of the Vesuvius eruption in AD 79. Some of the casts are so detailed, even facial expressions can be seen.

▼ Fully-dressed mummies line the walls of a church in Palermo, Italy. The dead wished to be preserved wearing their finest clothes.

79 **In the underground crypt of a church in Palermo, Sicily, are more than 2000 human mummies.** These are the bodies of local people, who were buried in the crypt more than 100 years ago. Instead of rotting away, the dry air has mummified their remains. Many of the mummies are propped against the walls, where they stand at odd angles, dressed in burial clothes.

80
The mummies of saints are displayed in many Roman Catholic churches. It isn't always the whole body that is on show, sometimes it is just a body part, called a 'relic'. Many of the mummies are natural, and are the result of being in a dry environment for many years. A few are artificial, and have been preserved on purpose. However, the Catholic Church believes that some saints have been preserved by God, and are evidence of miracles.

▲ The body of Saint Bernadette Soubirous (1844–1879) at Lourdes, France. Her body was exhumed (dug up) from her grave three times, and had not decomposed. People believed that she had been preserved by God.

81
Mummies have been made on the island of Papua New Guinea for generations. When a person died, they were put into a squatting position and their body was left to dry in the sun, or smoke-dried over a fire. Because the body was preserved, islanders believed their dead relatives were still living with them.

82
In Japan, there are about 20 mummies of Buddhist priests. The mummy of Tetsumonkai is one of them. He died in 1829, and a few years before his death he started to prepare his body for mummification. He ate less, and stopped eating rice, barley, wheat, beans and millet, as he believed that they harmed the body. After he died, his fellow priests put him in a sitting position with his legs crossed, and then dried out his body.

◀ The mummy of Tetsumonkai. His fellow priests dried his body by placing burning candles around it.

Studying mummies

83 Until recently, mummies were studied by opening them up. Unwrapping Egyptian mummies was popular in the 1800s, and was often done in front of an audience. Thomas Pettigrew (1791–1865) was an English surgeon who unwrapped many mummies at this time. He wrote some of the finest books about Egyptian mummies.

▲ An audience looks on as a mummy is unwrapped in the 1800s. This process destroyed lots of historical evidence.

84 There is no need to open up mummies today. Instead, mummies are studied by taking X-rays of bones, while scans reveal soft tissue in great detail. Mummies can even be tested to work out which families they came from.

▼ A Polish scientist prepares a 3000-year-old Egyptian mummy for an X-ray.

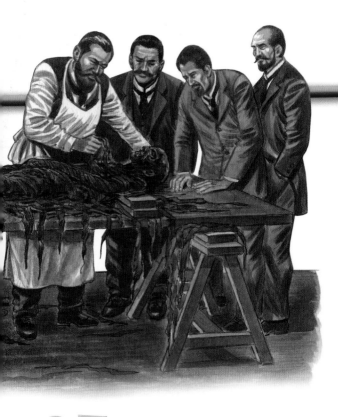

▶ This X-ray of a mummy's skull reveals that a fractured skull was the cause of death.

86 We can learn about the diseases and injuries people suffered by studying mummies.

Egyptian mummies have been studied the most. We can tell they had problems with their health. Gritty bread damaged their teeth, parasites (worms) entered their bodies when they drank polluted water, insect bites caused fevers, and hard work led to problems with their joints and bones.

85 French emperor Napoleon Bonaparte was fascinated by mummies.

After defeating the British in 1798, Napoleon and his troops became stranded in Egypt. With Napoleon were 150 scientists, who began to study Egypt and its mummies.

▼ When Napoleon left Egypt in 1799, he left behind a team of historians and scientists to study Egypt for him.

Animal mummies

87 **Animals were mummified in ancient Egypt, too!** Birds and fish were mummified as food for a dead person in the next life. Pet cats, dogs and monkeys became mummies so they could keep their dead owners company. Some bulls were believed to be holy as it was thought the spirits of the gods lived inside them. When they died, the bulls were mummified and buried in an underground tomb.

▲ Crocodiles were sacred to the Egyptian god Sobek. They were probably mummified in the same way as humans, then wrapped up.

▼ Red fur is still visible around the feet of Dima, the baby mammoth.

88 **A baby mammoth was found in the frozen ground of Siberia in 1977.** Many of these ancient elephant-like animals have been found in this part of Russia. What made this one special was the near-perfect state of its body. The animal was about a year old when it died, and was named Dima, after a stream close to where it was discovered.

89 **The world's oldest mummy is a dinosaur!** It is the fossil of an *Edmontosaurus*, which was found in Wyoming, USA, in 1908. This dinosaur died 65 million years ago, but instead of becoming a skeleton, its body was baked dry by the sun. When US fossil hunter Charles Sternberg discovered it, the skin and insides had been fossilized, as well as the bones.

▲ This frog was naturally mummified in 2006 when it died in a plant pot. The sun baked it dry.

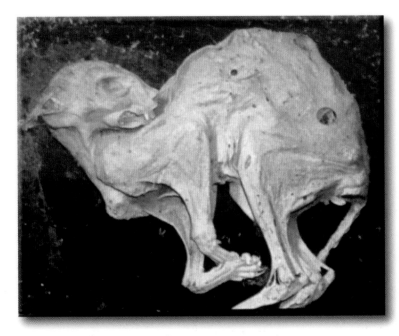

▲ This mummified cat was found in 1971 in Sudbury, Suffolk, UK. It had been walled up in an old mill to protect the building from harm.

90 **Cats have been made into mummies for thousands of years.** In ancient Egypt, cats were linked to the goddess, Bastet. They were bred to be killed as religious offerings at temples. Cat mummies are sometimes found behind the walls of old houses in Europe. It was believed a cat could bring good fortune, so a cat's body was sometimes walled up, after which it dried out until it was a natural mummy.

Mummy stories

91 The idea of the 'mummy's curse' started in 1923. A letter printed by a London newspaper said people would be cursed if they disturbed any pharaoh's tomb. Tutankhamun's tomb had just been found and people seemed to believe in curses. The letter seemed to confirm their fears. In fact, the entire thing was all made up!

▼ The opening of Tutankhamun's tomb by Howard Carter was the basis for the 'curse of the mummy'.

92 Mummies have not been used to make newspaper! There's a story that says linen was stripped from the mummies of Egypt, then used to make paper. The story goes on to say that an American newspaper was printed on this so-called 'mummy paper', sometime in the 1800s. It's a great story, but it's not true!

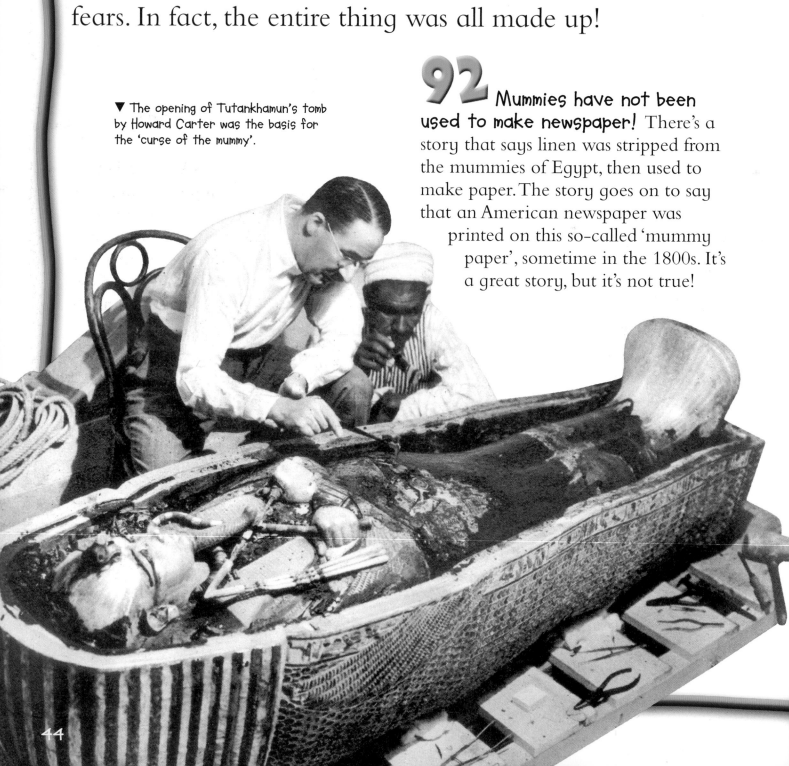

93

A mummy didn't sink *Titanic* in 1912! In the British Museum, London, is the lid of an Egyptian coffin. It is known as the 'Unlucky Mummy' as it's thought to be cursed. English journalist William Stead was on board *Titanic* when it sank. He told a story about the 'Unlucky Mummy' on the night the ship sank, and some people believed that this cursed the voyage.

▼ The 2001 film *The Mummy Returns* used lots of creepy special effects.

▼ A scene from the 1932 film *The Mummy*. Boris Karloff played the part of the mummy character, Im-Ho-Tep (left).

94

Mummies have become film stars. The first mummy film was made in 1909 and was called *The Mummy of King Rameses*. It was a black-and-white film without any sound. Many mummy films have been made since. One of the creepiest was *The Mummy*. It was made in 1932, and starred Boris Karloff.

95

As long ago as 1827, a book was written about a mummy. *The Mummy! A Tale of the Twenty-second Century* was written by Jane Loudon. The book was a science fiction story set in the year 2126. Lots more stories have been written about mummies since then – some for children. The author Jacqueline Wilson has even written *The Cat Mummy*, about a girl who tries to mummify her dead cat!

QUIZ

1. Was there a mummy on board *Titanic* ?
2. Which mummy film did Boris Karloff star in?
3. What started in 1923?
4. Who wrote *The Cat Mummy*?

Answers:
1. No 2. *The Mummy*
3. The mummy's curse
4. Jacqueline Wilson

Modern-day mummies

96 In Moscow, Russia, and in Beijing, China, modern-day mummies can be found. When Vladimir Ilich Lenin died in 1924, his body was mummified and put on display in Moscow. The same thing happened in China in 1976, when Mao Zedong died. Both men were leaders of their countries, and after they died, their bodies were preserved so that people could continue to see them.

▲ The mummy of Lenin is still on display in Moscow, Russia. The body was preserved using a secret technique.

97 The wife of a leader was also mummified. Eva Perón was the wife of the president of Argentina. After her death in 1952, her body was preserved. Then in 1955 the Argentine government was overthrown, and Eva's mummy was sent to Europe. It was returned to Argentina in 1974 to be buried.

I DON'T BELIEVE IT!

When the British artist Edward Burne-Jones found out that his paint was made from mummy remains, he buried the tube, and put daisies on the 'grave'!

98 An old man was mummified in America in 1994. A team of experts became the first people in modern times to mummify a human using ancient Egyptian techniques. They used the same tools as those used by the Egyptian mummy-makers. Then the organs were removed, the body was dried with natron and wrapped in linen.

99 If you have $67,000 (£35,500) to spare, you can have your dead body mummified! Odd as it sounds, there's a company in America that will carry out an Egyptian-style mummification on people. It's cheaper to have a cat or a dog mummified, and the smaller the pet, the less it costs!

100 Modern animal mummies have become works of art. English artist Damien Hirst has taken dead animals such as sheep, cows and sharks and preserved them with a special chemical. They have then been displayed to the public in art galleries as works of art.

▼ This preserved sheep was put on display in London by Damien Hirst in 1994.

Index

Contents

KT-441-399

A73607

Introduction

For the student

Welcome to *Just Listening and Speaking*. You can use this book with other students and a teacher, or you can work alone with it.

In this book, you will find 24 units and pronunciation exercises practising sounds, stress and intonation. Each unit has a section on listening and a section on speaking.

There are two accompanying CDs, containing the recordings for the 24 units and for the pronunciation exercises. Where you see the symbol ⏸, it means that you can listen to the CD. You will also find an Audioscript at the back of the book with all the recordings on the CDs.

When you see this symbol ⚷, it means that the answers to the practice exercises are in the Answer key at the back of the book. You can check your answers there.

We hope that this book helps you progress in English and, above all, that you enjoy using it.

For the teacher

This book is part of a series designed to be used alone or to supplement any course book you may be using. Each book in the series specialises in either language skills or aspects of the English language. It can be used either in class or by students working on their own.

Just Listening and Speaking consists of 24 units and pronunciation exercises. Each unit is divided into two sections. In the first section, students practise their listening skills. Topics are varied and include personal information, everyday actions, food and drink, describing a room or an area, telling a story, planning a party and taking part in radio shows.

The second section gives students the opportunity to practise speaking on a topic related to the first section. The activities are carefully graded and build up to role-plays, in which students interact with a 'partner' whose lines are recorded on the CD.

The pronunciation exercises, all recorded on the CDs, are divided into sounds, stress and intonation and are fully cross-referenced with the 24 units.

Students will be able to use the material without needing explanations or guidance on your part, and they can check their work using a comprehensive Answer key at the back of the book. However, the units and the pronunciation practice are also highly appropriate for work in class.

We hope you find this book a real asset and that you will also try the other books in the series: *Just Vocabulary*, *Just Reading and Writing* and *Just Grammar*.

WITHDRAWN

Just

Listening and Speaking

For class or self-study

Carol Lethaby
Ana Acevedo
Jeremy Harmer

Marshall Cavendish
Education

Photo acknowledgements

p.18 t ©Mike Watson Images/Corbis, b ©Rebecca Emery/Corbis; p.20 ©Timothy Tadder/Corbis; p.29 l ©Rick Gomez/Corbis, r ©Bloomimage/Corbis; p.30 ©Beathan/Corbis; p.49 a ©NASA/Getty Images, b ©2006 Research In Motion Limited, c ©Nicolas Asfouri/AFP/Getty Images; p.51 ©Dinodia Photo Library/Brand X/Corbis; p.52 ©John Lamb/Stone/Getty Images; p.55 ©Ariel Skelley/Corbis; p.59 ©Michele Constantini/PhotoAlto/Alamy; p.61 ©Hulton Archive/Getty Images; p.66 ©Altrendo Images/Getty Images

© 2007 Marshall Cavendish Education
Reprinted 2008, 2009

First published 2007 by Marshall Cavendish Education
Marshall Cavendish Education is a member of the Times Publishing Group

ISBN: 978-0-462-00042-8

Marshall Cavendish Education
5th Floor
32–38 Saffron Hill
London
EC1N 8FH

Designed by Hart McLeod, Cambridge

Printed and bound by Times Offset (M) Sdn Bhd

●A Listening Who are you?

1 Look at the pictures. The people are meeting for the first time. Read the conversations *a–d*.

a

Claudio, this is ....

Hi Frank. Pleased to meet you.

Nice to meet you too.

Conversation ....

b

Hello. I'm Cecilia. What's your name?

I'm .... , Frank Lewis. How are you?

Conversation ....

c

Hello. My name's Claudio.

I'm *Cecilia* . Nice to meet you, Claudio.

Conversation ......1......

d

Paula, this is Cecilia. And this is ....

Nice to meet you both.

Hi .... How are you?

Not bad, thank you.

Conversation ....

2 Listen to Track 1. Number the conversations in the pictures *a–d* in the order you hear them.

3 Listen to Track 1 again. Write the names you hear in the spaces in the conversations.

Claudio   Cecilia   Paula   Frank

T

●●●B Speaking Saying hello

1 Complete the table with phrases from the conversations on page 5.

Greetings	Introductions	Responses
Hello.	I'm (+ *name*).	Pleased to meet you.
(a)	(b) .... (+ *name*).	(d) ....
	(c) .... (+ *name*).	(e) .... ?

2 Meet Jo. Complete the conversation. Choose phrases from the table above.

Hello. (a) ....
(b) .... , Jo.

Hi! I'm Jo. What's your name?

Nice to meet you too.

3 Listen to Track 2 and speak after the beep. Use your conversation in Activity 2.

4 Have a conversation with Helena and Marco.

HELENA: Hello. I'm Helena. What's your name?

YOU: My name's ....

HELENA: Nice to meet you.

YOU: ....

HELENA: This is my friend Marco.

YOU: ....

MARCO: Hi. How are you?

YOU: ....

5 Listen to Track 3 and speak after the beep. Use your conversation in Activity 4.

●A Listening Greetings

1 Listen to Track 4. Tick (✓) the phrases when you hear them.

Greeting	Question	Response
Hi. Inf	How are you?	I'm very well, thank you.
Hello.	How's it going?	Fine, thanks.
Good morning. ✓		Very well, thanks.
Good afternoon.		Fine, thank you.
Good evening.		Not bad, thanks.
		And you?
		You?

2 Listen to Track 4 again. Match <u>three</u> conversations with pictures *a–c*.

Example: *a* − *S*

3 Listen to Track 4 again. Mark the phrases in the table in Activity 1 *F* (formal, for people you don't know well) or *Inf* (informal, for friends and colleagues).

B Speaking Hi! Where are you from?

1 Complete the conversations.

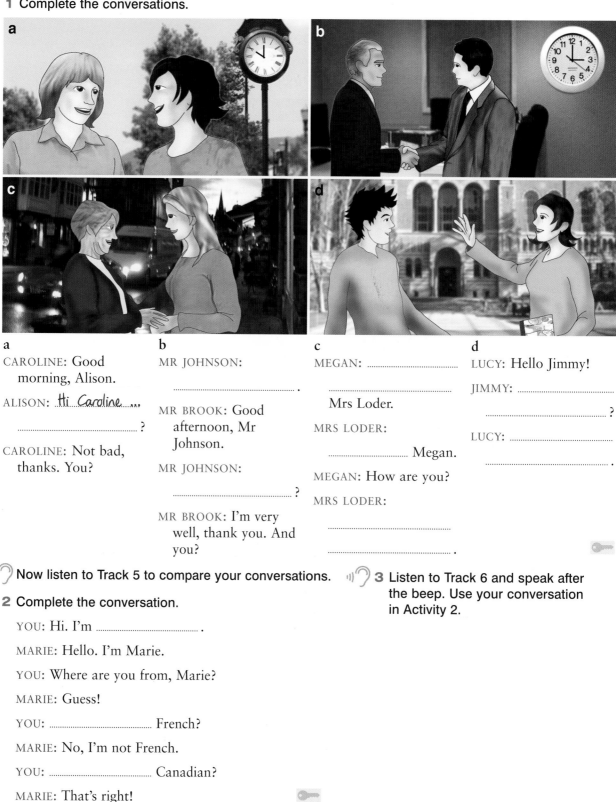

a
CAROLINE: Good
morning, Alison.

ALISON: Hi Caroline

.... ?

CAROLINE: Not bad,
thanks. You?

b
MR JOHNSON:

....

MR BROOK: Good
afternoon, Mr
Johnson.

MR JOHNSON:

.... ?

MR BROOK: I'm very
well, thank you. And
you?

c
MEGAN: ....

....
Mrs Loder.

MRS LODER:

.... Megan.

MEGAN: How are you?

MRS LODER:

....

....

d
LUCY: Hello Jimmy!

JIMMY: ....

.... ?

LUCY: ....

....

Now listen to Track 5 to compare your conversations.

2 Complete the conversation.

YOU: Hi. I'm ....

MARIE: Hello. I'm Marie.

YOU: Where are you from, Marie?

MARIE: Guess!

YOU: .... French?

MARIE: No, I'm not French.

YOU: .... Canadian?

MARIE: That's right!

3 Listen to Track 6 and speak after
the beep. Use your conversation
in Activity 2.

➡ Pronunciation Exercises B, Exercises 1–3

● A Listening Numbers

1 Work out the missing numbers. Clue: *fourteen* is regular and the missing numbers are regular too.

oh/zero (0) one (1) two (2) three (3) four (4) five (5) six (6) seven (7) eight (8) nine (9)

ten (10) eleven (11) twelve (12) thirteen (13) fourteen (14) fifteen (15) .... (16)

.... (17) eighteen (18) .... (19) twenty (20)

Listen to Track 7, check your answers and repeat the numbers.

2 Bingo Write any number between 0 and 20 in each box. Listen to Track 8 and tick (✓) the numbers as you hear them. When all your numbers are ticked, say *Bingo!* You win!

3 Listen to Track 9. Write the telephone numbers.

a   ....0208 495 3497..........

b   ....

c   ....

d   ....

4 Listen to the email addresses on Track 10. Label the items with the correct word, *at*, *dot* or *underscore*.

.... *dot* ....

a marilou@yahoo.com   b mari_lou@yahoo.co.uk

What's your email address? Practise saying it aloud.

➡ Pronunciation Exercises A, Exercises 1–3

●●●B Speaking Personal information

🔊 **1** A student is phoning a language school. Listen to the telephone conversation on Track 11. Complete this form with the words that you hear.

Just Right **School of English**   **Request for information**

First name: **(a)** _Maria_

Last name: **(b)** ....

Nationality: **(c)** ....

Email address: **(d)** ....

Telephone number: **(e)** ....

🔊 **2** Listen to Track 11 again. Complete the information.

Asking for personal information
Name: **(a)** .... ? Nationality: **(b)** .... ?
Email: *Do you have email?* (Email) address: *What's your (email) address?*
Asking for spelling: *How do you spell (that)?* Telephone number: **(c)** .... ?

3 You work for the *Just Right* School of English. Complete the conversation.

YOU: _Hello, the Just Right School of English!_

STUDENT: Can you give me some information please?

YOU: ....

STUDENT: Claire Baudson.

YOU: ....

STUDENT: B – A – U – D – S – O – N.

YOU: .... ?

STUDENT: I'm French.

YOU: .... ?

STUDENT: c.baudson@mynet.co.uk

YOU: .... ?

STUDENT: 03850 09486. It's my mobile phone.

YOU: _Thanks. I'll send you the information immediately._

STUDENT: Thanks. Bye.

🔊 **4** Listen to Track 12 and speak after the beep. Use your conversation in Activity 3.

UNIT 4

A Listening Who are they?

1 Label the pictures of the six people with words from the table.

Skin	Hair			Eyes
fair	long	black	straight	blue
dark	short	brown	curly	green
olive		blonde		black
		red		brown
		grey		

fair —

Zack Jones

Olivia Stott

Miriam Okyere

Joseph Smith

Susan Lee

Kenny Williams

2 Describe a member of your family. Write sentences describing their skin, their hair and their eyes.

Example: My sister has dark skin. She has long brown hair. It is very straight ...

3 Match the babies with the six adults in Activity 1. Write sentences.

Example: The baby in picture a is Susan Lee.

a

b

c

d

e

f

4 Listen to Track 13. Two friends are matching the babies and the adults. Write the letters you hear.

The baby in picture ....a..... is Susan Lee.

The baby in picture .... is Joseph Smith.

The baby in picture .... is Miriam Okyere.

The baby in picture .... is Zack Jones.

The baby in picture .... is Olivia Stott.

The baby in picture .... is Kenny Williams.

5 Listen to Track 14. Check your sentences in Activity 3. How many correct matches have you got? And the friends on the recording?

– number of names I guessed: ....

– number of names the friends guessed: ....

●●●B Speaking Describing yourself

1 Who do you look like, your father or your mother? Write sentences.

Example: My hair is straight, like my mother's hair.

2 Invent a new look for yourself. Write a short description of yourself for an Internet site.

Example: My name's ... I'm from ... I'm ... years old.
I have long blonde hair. It's curly. My eyes are blue and my skin is fair.

....

....

....

....

....

3 You make a new friend on the Internet. Complete the conversation.

JOAN: Hi. I'm Joan. What's your name?

YOU: ....

JOAN: Where are you from?

YOU: .... And you?

JOAN: I'm from Manchester, England. Tell me what you look like. Is your hair short or long?

YOU: ....

JOAN: My hair is dark and short. Is your hair dark too?

YOU: ....

JOAN: My eyes are brown. What about your eyes? What colour are they?

YOU: ....

JOAN: Send me a photo. Talk to you again soon. Bye!

YOU: ....

4 Listen to Track 15 and speak after the beep. Use your conversation in Activity 3.

●A Listening Going places

1 Look at the pictures. Where can you see these things, in picture A or in picture B?
Write A or B next to each word.

a airport   [B]
b ticket   [   ]
c platform   [   ]
d train station [   ]
e plane   [   ]
f suitcase   [   ]
g rucksack   [   ]

2 Look at pictures A and B carefully. Where are the people going? Write the destination in the table.

At the train station			
	Destination	Time	Platform
1	Clapham Junction		
2			
At the airport			
	Destination	Flight number	Gate
3		308	13A
4			
5			

3 Listen to five announcements on Track 16. Complete the information in the table in Activity 2.

Which passenger is Julian Jones? [   ]

4 Do you prefer to travel by plane, by train or by car? Why? Write a sentence.
Use the words in the box.

comfortable   fast   fun   interesting   quick   relaxing

Example: I prefer to travel by plane. It's fast and comfortable.

●●●B Speaking Talking about your everyday actions

1 When do you do these things? Write the day of the week in the table.

	Weekdays (Monday, Tuesday, Wednesday, Thursday, Friday)	Weekends (Saturday and Sunday)
Work	Monday to Friday	Saturday
Do sport		
Meet friends		
Go to the cinema		
Watch television		
Go shopping		

2 Read the conversation in Activity 3. How does Jo say *I really like* … ? How does she say *I really don't like* … ?

3 Talk to Jo about your everyday actions. Complete the conversation. Use actions from Activity 1.

JO: Today is Monday. I hate Mondays! Do you like Mondays?

YOU: ....

JO: What do you do on weekdays?

YOU: *(write two actions)* ....

....

JO: What's your favourite day of the week?

YOU: ....

JO: Why?

YOU: *(write two actions)* ....

.... What about you?

JO: My favourite day is Saturday. I go shopping and I meet my friends. I love Saturdays!

4 Listen to Track 17 and speak after the beep. Use your conversation in Activity 3.

•A Listening Food and drink

1 Write *yes* next to the foods you eat or drink. Write *no* next to the things you never eat or drink. Label the foods with words from the box.

> bread   cake   cheese   chicken   fruit   hamburgers
> ice cream   milk   orange juice   tea   vegetables

yes

a ....*cheese*....

b ....

c ....

d ....

e ....

no

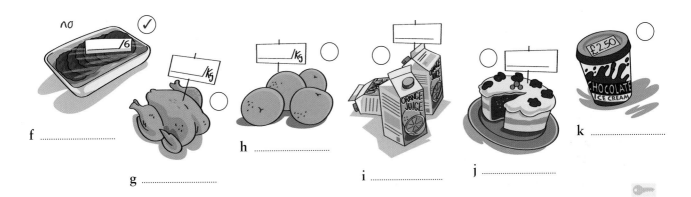

f ....

g ....

h ....

i ....

j ....

k ....

2 Listen to the radio ads on Track 18. Which ad is for a supermarket, 1, 2 or 3? Tick (✓) the correct ad.

Ad 1 [ ]   Ad 2 [ ]   Ad 3 [ ]

3 Listen to Track 18 again. Look at the pictures *f–k* in Activity 1. Which things are on offer at Food Mart this week? Tick (✓) the correct pictures. Write the prices on the signs.

4 You have £10 to buy things at the supermarket. What do you want to buy? How much or how many?

Example: I want to buy two chocolate cakes and six hamburgers for only £9.50!

●●●B Speaking How good is your diet?

1 Choose the menu you like best for each meal. Then check your score.

Menu 1
Breakfast orange juice, fruit and cheese
Lunch salad, a sandwich, fruit and water
Dinner fish, vegetables, fruit and water

Menu 2
Breakfast coffee, bread and meat
Lunch a sandwich, crisps and a coke
Dinner meat, bread, chocolate cake or ice cream

You choose ...	Your diet is ...
menu 1 for each meal	= very healthy.
menu 1 for two meals	= OK but you can eat better!
menu 2 for each meal	= terrible! Eat more fruit and vegetables!

2 Write questions for a questionnaire.

Questionnaire: You and Food

a eat / snacks
   Do you eat snacks?

b eat / fish / twice a week
   .... ?

c drink / eight glasses of water / every day?
   .... ?

d eat / hamburgers / every day
   .... ?

e have / ice cream / often
   .... ?

f drink / three cups of coffee or tea / every day))
   .... ?

➠ Pronunciation Exercises C, Exercises 1 and 2

3 You ask a woman in the street the questions on your questionnaire. Complete the conversation. Use your questionnaire from Activity 2.

WOMAN: Hi!

YOU: _Can I ask you some questions for a_
     questionnaire?

WOMAN: Sure.

YOU: .... ?

WOMAN: Snacks? Like crisps and sweets? Sure. I love snacks!

YOU: .... ?

WOMAN: I don't eat hamburgers every day but I eat meat every day.

YOU: .... ?

WOMAN: Eight glasses? I probably drink about 12, or more!

YOU: .... ?

WOMAN: Well, I don't like fish so I never eat it.

YOU: .... ?

WOMAN: I have a cup of tea in the morning but I don't drink coffee.

YOU: .... ?

WOMAN: Mmm. Yes! I love ice cream, especially chocolate. So, do I eat well or badly?

YOU: (*choose one answer*)
     You eat very well! /
     Sorry. You eat very badly!

4 Listen to Track 19 and speak after the beep. Use your conversation in Activity 3.

··A Listening What's on at the cinema?

1 Look at the posters *a–d* on the right. Write what type of film they are. Then write a list of your four favourite films.
Match the films and the type of film.

My favourite films	Types of film
....	horror film
....	action film
....	romantic film
....	western
....	comedy

What's your favourite type of film? ....

a ⚷ action film ....

b ....

2 Listen to Track 20 and match the titles of the films with the posters in Activity 1.

Small Adventures	[c]
Terror in London	[ ]
Always	[ ]
Today's Hero	[ ]

⚷ c ....

d ....

3 Listen to Track 20 again and complete the information.

The Odeon Cinema – This week! 56 Park St

Screen Number	Name of film	Information	Times
(a)	*Small Adventures*	For all the (b)	1 p.m., (c) ....,
(d)	*Terror in London*	For people over (e) .... years old	7 p.m., (f) ....
(g)	(h)	Romantic comedy for people of (i) .... ages	3.30 p.m., (j) ...., ...
(k)	(l)	Action (m) .... with Harry Murray	(n) ...., 6 p.m., ...

Which is the best film for you? .... ⚷

• • B Speaking Guess who!

➠ Pronunciation Exercises C, Exercises 3 and 4

1 Read the files on Rowena and Rhonda. Are these things the same (S) or different (D)?

a their home town   ....S....

b their initials   ....

c their likes   ....

d their hobbies   ....

e their jobs   ....

2 Play a guessing game with Jo. Jo chooses a picture. You ask questions and guess who she is, Rowena or Rhonda. Write questions to complete the conversation.

Name: Rowena Robertson

Lives in: Hollywood, California

Likes: cinema (favourite film: *The Queen*)

Hobby: collecting autographs

Job: selling tickets in cinema

Name: Rhonda Roberts

Lives in: Hollywood, California

Likes: cinema (favourite film: *The Queen*)

Hobby: collecting photographs

Job: actor

JO: I'm ready to play. Ask your first question.

YOU: (where / live / do / you / ?)

.... ?

JO: I live in California.

YOU: (you / do / live / in Hollywood / ?)

.... ?

JO: Yes, I do live in Hollywood.

YOU: (the cinema / like / do / you / ?)

.... ?

JO: Yes, I do. I love films.

YOU: (favourite film / what / is / your / ?)

.... ?

JO: My favourite film is *The Queen*. It's about the queen of England.

YOU: (hobby / have / you / do / a / ?)

OK. .... ?

JO: A hobby? Yes, I collect autographs of famous film stars.

YOU: (work / you / in a cinema / do / ?)

.... ?

JO: Yes, I do. But I'm not an actor. I sell the tickets!

YOU: (you / are / ... / ?)

.... ?

JO: That's right! My turn now. Here is my first question …

3 Listen to Track 21 and ask your questions after the beep. Use your conversation in Activity 2.

••A Listening Ouch! It hurts!

1 Look at the pictures. Label the parts of the body with words from the box.

| arm | foot | hand | head | leg | stomach |

head

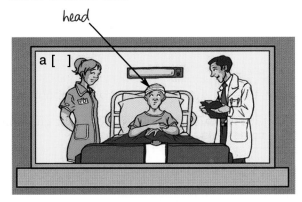

a [ ]

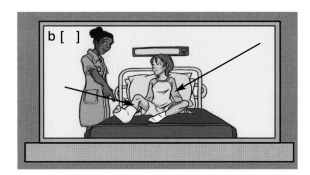

b [ ]

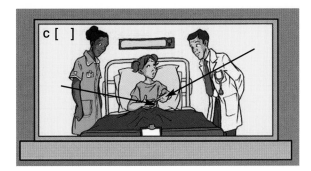

c [ ]

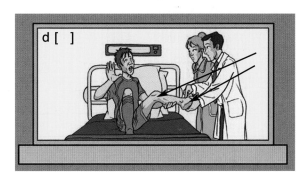

d [ ]

2 Listen to <u>three</u> scenes in a hospital on Track 22. Number three of the scenes in Activity 1 in the order you hear them.

3 Now complete the table.

Middletown General Hospital		
Name	**Room number**	**What's the matter?**
Jimmy	(a)	(b)
(c)	8	(d)
(e)	(f)	Her stomach hurts.

4 Listen to Track 22 again. How does the doctor say these things? Complete the words.

a I'm coming immediately.

→ I'll be right t____ , nurse.

b Look after Jimmy.

→ T___ c___ of Jimmy.

c What's the problem?

→ W___'s the m _____?

d I want to look (at your leg).

→ L__ me s__.

●●B Speaking What's the matter?

1 You're a doctor. How do you respond in these situations? Write a response.

   a A patient phones and says, 'Come quickly. I have a problem.'

     YOU: _I'll be ..._____ .

   b Your patient looks ill. She's covering her eyes with her hands.

     YOU: _____ ?

   c Your patient says, 'It's my eye. It hurts!'

     YOU: _____ .

2 You are not feeling well. You go to see the doctor. Tick (✓) the things that are true about you.

	often	sometimes	occasionally	never
My head hurts.				
I feel tired.				
I have a lot of work.				
I use a computer at work.				
I listen to music.				
I do exercise.				
I laugh.				
I watch television.				

3 Complete the conversation with the information in the table in Activity 2.

DOCTOR: What's the matter?

YOU: _____ .

DOCTOR: Tell me about your job. Do you have a lot of work?

YOU: _____ .

DOCTOR: Do you use a computer at work?

YOU: _____ .

DOCTOR: How often do you exercise?

YOU: _____ .

DOCTOR: Do you eat a good breakfast?

YOU: _____ .

DOCTOR: What do you do to relax?

YOU: _____ .

DOCTOR: Hmm. I think you need to relax more often. You will feel better soon.

YOU: _Thank you doctor._____ .

> **Just note**
> The adverb of frequency goes <u>before</u> the verb.
> *I **sometimes** go for a walk.*
> Not: *I go sometimes for a walk.*

4 Listen to Track 23 and speak after the beep. Use your conversation in Activity 3.

•A Listening A radio advertisement

1 Look at the table. Which of the clothes do you wear? When? Write true sentences.

	always		jeans	trousers	to work / to school.
	usually		(shorts)	a skirt	in summer.
I	often	wear	a suit	a dress	at weekends.
	sometimes		a shirt	a T-shirt	to parties.
	never		shoes	sandals	when I go out at night.
			trainers		when I see my boy / girlfriend.

Example: *I often wear a skirt to work.*

2 Look at the picture. Which clothes in the table in Activity 1 are NOT in the picture? Circle the clothes in the table.

(a) *dresses* ....

£19.99

In black and (b) ....

T-shirts

(c) £ ....

S, M, (d) ....

Suits

(e) £ ....

Colour: (f) ....

Casual (h) ....

£9.99

Sizes: S, (i) .... ,

(j) .... , XL

For summer

(g) ....

only £14.99

3 Listen to a radio advertisement on Track 24. Which clothes are in the picture in Activity 2 <u>and</u> in the advertisement? Tick (✓) them as you hear them.

4 Listen to Track 24 again and complete the information on the signs *a–j* in the picture.

➡ Pronunciation Exercises A, Exercises 18 and 19

●●B Speaking What shall we take?

1 You are going on a two-day camping trip with a friend. The weather is cold. Write a shopping list for your trip. You have £200 in total.

Entertainment

MP3 player	£50
CD player	£35
mobile phone	£30
CDs	£10

Food (for two people)

bread	£3
eggs	£3
chicken	£15
milk	£5
coffee	£5
tea	£4
salad	£15
meat	£20
vegetables	£15

Clothes (for two people)

warm jacket	£20
boots	£20

2 Complete the conversations a–f with the expressions in the table.

✓	✗	?
Great! That's a good idea! OK, that's fine.	That's not a good idea! What a terrible idea!	Hmm. I'm not sure about that.

a A: I want to take a mobile phone.

B: (✓) ....

b A: I want to spend more money. What do you think?

B: (?) ....

c A: How about a computer?

B: (✗) ....

d A: Let's take some hamburgers.

B: (✓) ....

e A: I want to buy an MP3 player.

B: (✓) ....

f A: I want to take some sandals.

B: (✗) ....

Now listen to Track 25 and check your answers.

3 You are telling your friend about your shopping list. Complete the conversation.

YOUR FRIEND: OK, what do you want to take for entertainment, for fun?

YOU: ....

YOUR FRIEND: OK, that's fine. But I want to take lots of CDs too. What do you think?

YOU: ....

YOUR FRIEND: OK. What about food?

YOU: ....

YOUR FRIEND: Hmm. I'm not sure about that. What about clothes? I want to take my new dress.

YOU: ....

YOUR FRIEND: All right. What about the money? How much is it for all that?

YOU: ....

YOUR FRIEND: That's fine. But it's very cold now. How about going camping in the summer when the weather is warm?

YOU: ....

4 Listen to Track 26 and speak after the beep. Use your conversation in Activity 3.

● A Listening What's happening?

1 Look at the pictures. Label the pictures with the sentences below.

a The band is playing.
b The child is dancing.
c The people are watching and clapping.
d The people are wearing uniforms.

1 [ ]

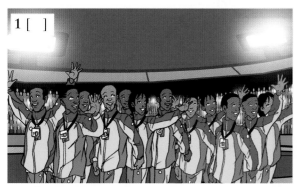

...... The people ....

2 [✓]

......

3 [ ]

4 [ ]

......

2 Listen to a commentary on Track 27. Tick (✓) the pictures the speakers are describing.

Which picture do the speakers NOT talk about?

......

3 Listen to Track 27 again. Complete the sentences with the words you hear.

a It's a b.............. d.............. for the carnival here at Notting Hill.

b Yes, i.......... i.........., Sue. A perfect day! The s.......... is shining.

c Here comes the next b................. It's the Children's Brixton Group. They're wearing fantastic c.................., erm, costumes. Fabulous colours: y.............. , r.............. , g.............. , b.............. .

d And l.............. to that m..............!

e Yes, the band i.............. p.............. calypso music.

4 Look at the picture that is <u>not</u> the carnival. Answer the questions.

a Where are the people? *in a stadium*

b Who are they? ....

c What are they wearing? ....

d What are they doing? ....

e What time of day is it? ....

Now use your answers to write a short radio commentary. Listen to Track 27 again for help.

Example: *You are listening to Radio Sports. We are at the opening ceremony of the Olympic games. It's a beautiful night...*

5 Read your commentary aloud.

➡ Pronunciation Exercises A, Exercises 12–15

●●● B Speaking Let's find the differences!

1 Look at the picture. Write the names of the people in the spaces.

a ....Tom....'s riding a bike.

b .... and .... are playing baseball.

c ....'s walking.

d .... is running.

e ....'s playing the guitar.

f ....'s listening to Nicky.

g ....'s climbing a tree.

h .... and .... are dancing. 🔑

2 Listen to Track 28 and check your answers. Underline the words that are stressed. (Clue: they sound louder.)

Example: _Tom's riding a bike._

3 Help Lenny find the differences between your picture and his picture. Look at the picture in Activity 1 and complete the conversation.

LENNY: Have you got five young men, Alex, Sam, Nicky, Andy and Tom?

YOU: _Yes, I have_ .

LENNY: Is Alex running?

YOU: _Yes, he is_ .

LENNY: Is Tom lying on the grass?

YOU: ....

LENNY: OK. That's one difference. What's Andy doing?

YOU: ....

LENNY: He's driving a car in my picture. So that's two differences. Is Nicky listening to Anna? She's playing the guitar.

YOU: .... He's

....

LENNY: Aha! Two more differences. What's Sam doing?

YOU: ....

LENNY: Have you got five young women, Mia, Jill, Tina, Katie and Anna?

YOU: ....

LENNY: What are they doing?

YOU: Tina and Katie .... ;

Mia's .... ;

Jill ....

and Anna ....

LENNY: So only Anna is different. How many differences do we have?

YOU: ....

LENNY: Great! That was fun. 🔑

4 Listen to Track 29 and speak after the beep. Use your conversation in Activity 3.

•A Listening Fashion

1 Look at the pictures of a fashion show. Write a list of clothes and a list of adjectives in the table.

clothes	adjectives
suit dress	green

a [ ] b [1] c [ ] d [ ]

2 Listen to Track 30. Number the pictures *a–d* in Activity 1 in the order of the recording.

3 Listen to Track 30 again. Tick (✓) your words in Activity 1 if you hear them.

4 What do you think about the clothes? Do you agree with the people on Track 30? Complete the table. Listen to Track 30 again if you want.

Clothes	Your opinion	Their opinion
Dress by Enzo Muriatti		
Suit by Abel Schmitt		
Casual trousers and sweater		Not very original
Suit by Anna Jacobs		

●●● B Speaking Describing people

1 What do the people look like? Describe the people in the pictures.
Use words from the box and other words you know.

Example: *Maria is tall and slim. She has brown hair. She's wearing black trousers, a blue jacket and boots. She's beautiful.*

Don ....

....

Daniel ....

....

Monica ....

....

Richard ....

....

> tall/short
> thin/fat
> slim/chubby
> beautiful/plain (women)
> handsome/unattractive (men)
> elegant
> fashionable

Maria   Don   Daniel   Monica   Richard

2 Write the questions in the box in the correct space.

> How tall is he/she?
> What's his/her hair like?
> What is he/she wearing?
> What does he/she look like?

a A: How tall is ... . ?

B: She's short. About 1.50m, I think.

b A: .... ?

B: A black dress and black boots.

c A: .... ?

B: She's tall and slim.

d A: .... ?

B: It's black, short and curly.

➠ Pronunciation Exercises B, Exercise 6

3 Play a guessing game with Jamie. Ask and answer questions to identify the people in Activity 1. Complete the conversation.

JAMIE: Let's play a game. You choose one of the people and I guess who it is, OK? How tall is the person?

YOU: ....

JAMIE: What does the person look like?

YOU: ....

JAMIE: What's he or she wearing?

YOU: ....

JAMIE: Is it Monica?

YOU: ....

JAMIE: OK. Your turn now. You ask the questions.

YOU: .... ?

JAMIE: Very tall. About 1.80m, I think.

YOU: .... ?

JAMIE: Well, tall and thin with short red curly hair.

YOU: .... ?

JAMIE: Guess!

YOU: .... ?

JAMIE: Yes, he's wearing a brown suit.

YOU: .... ?

JAMIE: That's right!

4 Listen to Track 31 and speak after the beep. Use your conversation in Activity 3.

A Listening Phone messages

1 What form of communication do you use in these situations? Write the words in the spaces.

email   fax   letter   phone call

a You are a bank manager. You want to tell a client something important about his bank account. ......*letter*......

b You work in a bookshop. You want to tell a client his order is in the shop. ....

c You want to tell a group of friends about your new email address. ....

d You work in an office. You want to send a client some papers.

....

2 Listen to a telephone conversation between Cath and Tim on Track 32. True (T), False (F) or Don't Know (DK)?

a Cath works in an office.   [T]

b Martha is at the shops.   [   ]

c Cath offers to phone Martha.   [   ]

d Tim wants to see Martha that day.   [   ]

e Tim's call is about work.   [   ]

f Tim tells Cath some important times.   [   ]

3 Listen to Track 32 again. Who says these things, Tim or Cath? Write the name in the spaces.

a Hello?   ....*Cath*............

b Can I speak to Martha, please?   ....

c Can I take a message?   ....

d I'm sending her a fax for Mr Roberts.   ....

e OK. Don't worry. I'll tell her.   ....

4 Listen to Track 32 again. Complete the message for Martha.

Message for: Martha Higgins   Date/Time: 12/05 12 o'clock
From: Tim Franklin   Message taken by: (your name)

1 Tim's sending a ....fax........ for ....
2 meeting with .... at ....
3 meet .... at .... o'clock at ....

5 Listen to Track 33. Listen to Cath and Martha. Complete the message from Cath to Martha.

Message for: Martha Higgins   Date/Time: 12/05 12 o'clock
From: Tim Franklin   Message taken by: Cath

1 Tim's sending a .... for ....the...........................
2 meeting with .... at ....
3 meet .... for .... at .... o'clock .

What are Cath's four mistakes?

a ....
b ....
c ....
d ....

●●●B Speaking Communication

1 Look at these sentences. Are they true or false for you? Put a
tick (✓) or a cross (✗).

a I often use a computer.   [   ]

b I often use the Internet.   [   ]

c I write emails to friends and for business.   [   ]

d I write emails for work.   [   ]

e I use a mobile phone for important things.   [   ]

f I use my mobile phone to talk to friends.   [   ]

g I have a web page.   [   ]

h I write cards and letters to friends and family.   [   ]

2 You are answering a questionnaire on the phone. Complete the
conversation. Use the information in Activity 1.

INTERVIEWER: Hello? We are doing a survey about technology
and communication. Can you answer some questions?

YOU: _Sure._ ....

INTERVIEWER: Do you use a computer?

YOU: ....

INTERVIEWER: What do you use your computer for?

YOU: ....

INTERVIEWER: Do you send emails to friends and family or only
for work?

YOU: ....

INTERVIEWER: Do you ever write cards or letters?

YOU: ....

INTERVIEWER: Right. What about your mobile phone? When do
you use your mobile phone?

YOU: ....

INTERVIEWER: One last question. Do you have a web page?

YOU: ....

INTERVIEWER: Why?

YOU: ....

INTERVIEWER: Well, that's it. Thank you very much for your
help.

YOU: ....

3 Listen to Track 34 and speak after the beep. Use your
conversation in Activity 3.

●A Listening Lost and found

1 Label the pictures with the prepositions.

between   in   near   next to   on   opposite   under

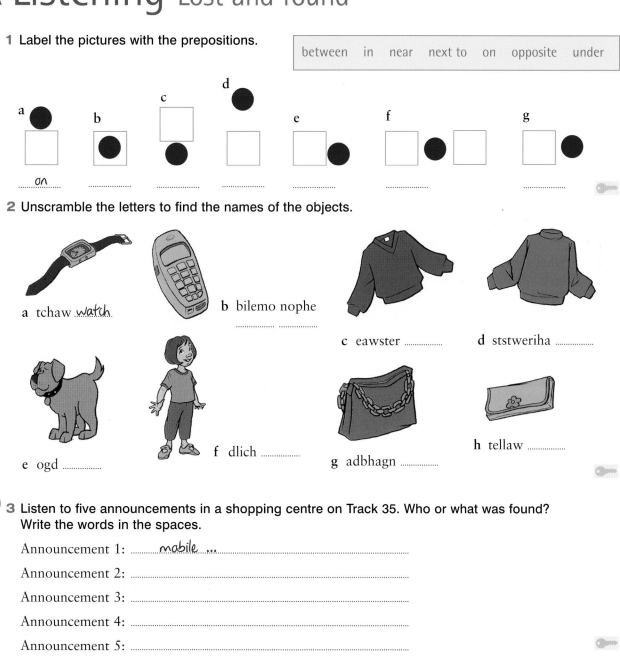

a ...on...   b ....   c ....   d ....   e ....   f ....   g ....

2 Unscramble the letters to find the names of the objects.

a tchaw ..watch.

b bilemo nophe ....

c eawster ....

d ststweriha ....

e ogd ....

f dlich ....

g adbhagn ....

h tellaw ....

3 Listen to five announcements in a shopping centre on Track 35. Who or what was found? Write the words in the spaces.

Announcement 1: ....mobile....

Announcement 2: ....

Announcement 3: ....

Announcement 4: ....

Announcement 5: ....

4 Listen to Track 35 again. Write *1–5* where they were found.

a under a restaurant table   [1]

b on a restaurant table   [   ]

c in the supermarket   [   ]

d next to the supermarket   [   ]

e near the toy store   [   ]

f in the toy store   [   ]

g in the bank   [   ]

h near the bank   [   ]

i on the bookstore counter   [   ]

j under the bookstore counter   [   ]

5 You found something in the shopping centre. Write an announcement.
Listen to Track 35 again if you want.

Example: We found a blue and black wallet on the table at Moonbeam Café. Please come to the Information Desk to get it.

••• B Speaking Describing a room

1 What's your bedroom like? What are your favourite things? Write sentences using the nouns and adjectives in the table.

nouns
bed bedside table chair computer curtains desk lamp rug television

adjectives
beautiful big comfortable modern new nice old small colour adjectives, e.g. red

Example: My room is small but nice. I've got a comfortable bed, ...

2 This is your new living room. Write six sentences about the furniture in the room.

Example: I've got a big sofa next to the window.

I've got a small lamp on the small table.

3 Listen to the questions on Track 36. Look at the picture of your room in Activity 2. Write your answers to the questions.

a QUESTION: Have you got any sofas in your living room?

Yes, I have. I've got two sofas.

b QUESTION:

YOU:_____ .

c QUESTION:

YOU:_____ .

d QUESTION:

YOU:_____ .

e QUESTION:

YOU:_____ .

f QUESTION:

YOU:_____ .

g QUESTION:

YOU:_____ .

4 Listen to Track 36 again and answer the questions after the beep.

5 Describe your new room to a friend. Complete the conversation.

YOUR FRIEND: You've got a new house? How exciting! What's your new living room like?

YOU:_____ .

YOUR FRIEND: Is there any furniture in the room?

YOU:_____ .

YOUR FRIEND: Where is the big sofa?

YOU:_____ .

YOUR FRIEND: And the small one? Where is the small sofa?

YOU:_____ .

YOUR FRIEND: And where's the small table?

YOU:_____ .

YOUR FRIEND: Where are the lamps?

YOU:_____ .

YOUR FRIEND: Have you got rugs in the room?

YOU:_____ .

YOUR FRIEND: Well, that sounds nice. Hey, what about the television? Where is the television?

YOU:_____ .

YOUR FRIEND: No television? That's not possible. A house without a television is not a home!

6 Listen to Track 37 and speak after the beep. Use your conversation in Activity 5.

7 Rearrange the furniture in your new living room. Add two things you would like to have in the room. Write sentences.

Example: *The big sofa is now opposite the window. I have a television and computer games.*

●●●A Listening A guided tour

1 Look at the pictures. Unscramble the words to find the names of the places.

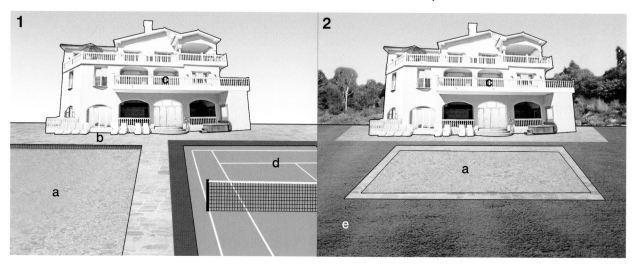

    a wisimmng loop .....Swimming..... ....

    b cartere ....

    c alconyb ....

    d sinnet trouc ....

    e dengra ....

2 Listen to a guided tour on Track 38. Look at the pictures in Activity 1. Which is Marlene's house, 1) or 2)?

3 Listen to Track 38 again. Are these sentences True (T) or False (F)?

    a The sofa is from Italy.   [F]

    b The house has 12 bedrooms.   [ ]

    c Each bedroom has a bathroom.   [ ]

    d Marlene's ten cooks all work together. [ ]

    e Marlene has two dining rooms.   [ ]

    f The swimming pool is always closed. [ ]

    g Local children sometimes come to the house. [ ]

4 Would you like to live in Marlene's house? Why or why not? Write two sentences.

Example: I would/wouldn't like to live in Marlene's house because...

⇒ **Pronunciation Exercises A, Exercises 20 and 21**

•B Speaking My home town

1 Complete the sentences with the names of the places.

a I'm going to the ....cinema........ to see the new James Bond film.

b I'm going to the .... to see a Shakespeare play.

c I don't want to cook. Let's go to a .... tonight.

d I like shopping at the .... : you can buy anything you want in the same place.

e There is nothing in the fridge. I have to go to the .... to buy some food.

f Which .... do your children go to?

g Karima is a doctor. She works in a ....

h Take the dog for a walk in the .... It can run there.

2 What's in your part of town or city? Complete the information in the table.

Places	How many?	Examples?
Supermarket	3	Super Food
Cinema		
Theatre		
Restaurant		
Shopping centre		
Hospital		
Park		
School		

3 Read the situations *a–c*. Is your town or city a good place for the people in the situations to live in?

    a The Johnsons are a family with young children. ....

    b Mr and Mrs Moore are 68 years old. They don't work any more. ....

    c Peter is a young architect. He loves going out and doing sport. ....

4 Tell your friend Lorna about your home town or city. Then ask her about her town. Complete the conversation.

LORNA: Where do you live?

YOU: ....

LORNA: Is it a good place to live?

YOU: ....

LORNA: Are there any places to go shopping?

YOU: ....

LORNA: What about entertainment? Are there any places for that?

YOU: ....

LORNA: Is it a good place for children?

YOU: .... because ....

LORNA: Is there anything special, like a large hospital or something?

YOU: ....

    .... ?

LORNA: My town? Well, it's very beautiful but very, very small.

YOU: .... ?

LORNA: A shopping centre? No, there isn't. There are only a few shops and there is no cinema!

YOU: .... ?

LORNA: Yes, it is a good place to live ... if you are 80 years old! 🔑

5 Listen to Track 39 and speak after the beep. Use your conversation in Activity 4.

•A Listening Listening to the radio

1 Match the types of programme and the titles.

Names of programmes	Type of programme	✓	Preferences
1 *Theatre at Home*	a the news		
2 *The World Today*	b the weather forecast		
3 *Phone and Tell*	c music programme		
4 *Top Ten Songs of the Week*	d sports programme		
5 *Come Rain or Sunshine*	e play		
6 *Football Champions League results*	f phone-in show		

Do you listen to the radio? Tick (✓) the types of programme you listen to.
Number the types of programme in order of preference (1 = favourite).

2 Listen to the radio programmes on Track 40. Write the type of programme.

Programme a: ....

Programme b: ....

Programme c: ....

Programme d: ....

3 Listen to the radio programmes on Track 40 again.
Are these sentences True (T) or False (F)?

a The Prime Minister is in France.   [T]

b The Prime Minister is talking to British businesspeople
   in Paris.   [ ]

c Liverpool played Chelsea. Chelsea won the match.   [ ]

d It's cold in the capital today.   [ ]

e The title of today's play is *Who let you out?*   [ ]

f Toby Grant is a character in the play.   [ ]

4 Listen to a radio programme on Track 41. What type of programme is it?

5 Listen to Track 41 again. Match the names with the pictures.

Susie   Kevin   Joanne   Jack   Brian

6 Listen to Track 41 again and match the date with the event.

a Kevin's birthday   April 2nd (2/4)
b Jack and Brian's birthday   April 3rd (3/4)
c wedding anniversary   April 4th (4/4)

7 Complete the sentences with the words or numbers you hear.

a You're ..... listening to ..... Radio Barrowtown, ... FM.

b My name's Susie Martin and I'll be with you for the next

.... hours, playing the songs you want to hear for

the people you .... !

c Dear Susie, I love your ....

and I'd like to hear a .... for my lovely wife, Joanne,

and our twin ....

d This is Lou Reed with *Perfect Day* for Kevin March and his

.... Joanne on their anniversary and for Jack and

Brian March on their .... Happy

.... and happy ....

•B Speaking A phone-in radio programme

1 You want to play a song on the radio for people you love. Complete the information in the table.

What song?	Who is it for?	On what special day?
a I Just Called to Say I Love You	Lucy	It's our anniversary.
b		
c		
d		
e		

2 You want to send a message with the songs to the people. Write the messages.

Example: To Lucy, I want to say 'Thank you' for the happy years.

3 You call a radio station to ask for a song for two of the people in Activity 1. Complete the conversation.

DJ: You are listening to YourTown Radio on 92.8 FM. Do you want us to play a special song for a special person? Phone now! … And here's our first caller. Hello? Who's calling?

YOU: ....

DJ: Where are you calling from?

YOU: ....

DJ: What song do you want to hear?

YOU: ....

DJ: Is this for a special person?

YOU: ....

DJ: Is it for a special occasion?

YOU: ....

DJ: What's your message?

YOU: ....

DJ: Great! Any other song you want to play?

YOU: ....

DJ: Who is it for?

YOU: ....

DJ: Any message? What do you want to say?

YOU: ....

DJ: That is lovely. Here are the songs – just for you.

4 Listen to Track 42 and speak after the beep. Use your conversation in Activity 3.

···A Listening Routines and timetables

1 When do you do these things? Write the times.

go to bed ....

finish work

have lunch   go to work   get up

....

2 Listen to some questions about your timetable on Track 43. Write answers to the questions.

a *I get up at ...*... .

b ....

c ....

d ....

e ....

f ....

3 Listen to Rob talking about his college timetable on Track 44.
Tick (✓) the subjects Rob studies.

chemistry [   ]   maths [   ]   physics [   ]   literature [   ]   music [   ]

biology [   ]   sports [   ]

What do you think Rob studies at college?

....

4 Listen to Track 44 again. Does Rob like his timetable? Why or why not?

....

5 Listen to Track 44 again and complete his timetable.

	9.00–11.00	11.00–1.00	1.00–5.00
M	biology		biology lab
T			
W			
Th			
F			

What do you think about Rob's timetable? Write a sentence.

....

•B Speaking A job interview

➡ Pronunciation Exercises A, Exercises 22 and 23

1 Answer the questions. Use *Yes, I can* or *No, I can't*.

a Can you speak English?   ....

b Can you use a computer?   ....

c Can you take phone messages?   ....

d Can you speak German?   ....

If you answered *Yes, I can* to more than two questions, then you can apply for the job below.

2 Prepare for your interview. What can you do? Write *Yes, I can* or *No, I can't*.

Activity	Can you do it?
Use a computer	
Use more than one computer programme	
Write business letters	
Send faxes	
Write reports	
Do presentations	
Speak English	
Speak a second foreign language	

3 You are at your interview. Complete the conversation.

INTERVIEWER: Hello, I'm Thomas Harvey.

YOU: ....

INTERVIEWER: Pleased to meet you too. Please sit down. Now, what computer programmes can you use?

YOU: ....

INTERVIEWER: All right. Can you write business letters?

YOU: ....

INTERVIEWER: For this job you have to talk to some people in English. How good is your English?

YOU: ....

INTERVIEWER: You don't have to speak another foreign language for the job but it is useful. Can you speak another language?

YOU: ....

INTERVIEWER: What other things can you do? Things that are important for this job, like writing reports.

YOU: ....

INTERVIEWER: Very well. Oh, just one more thing. Can you get up early? You must be here at 7.30.

YOU: ....

INTERVIEWER: Thank you for coming. Don't call us, we'll call you. Goodbye.

YOU: ....

4 Listen to Track 45 and speak after the beep. Use your conversation in Activity 3.

•A Listening A yoga class

1 Label the parts of the body
with words from the box.

> arm   back   chest   foot   head
> knee   leg   stomach   throat

arm

2 Look at these pictures of a woman doing yoga. Match the descriptions
1–5 with the pictures.

a   b   c   d   e

1 She's standing with her arms by her side.   [c]

2 She's holding her feet with her hands and looking up.   [   ]

3 She's on her knees with her arms up beside her body.   [   ]

4 She's on her knees.   [   ]

5 She's holding her left foot with her left hand.   [   ]

3 Listen to the instructions from the yoga teacher on Track 46. Answer these questions.

a What is the name of the yoga pose? ....

b Which three words in the box in Activity 1 are <u>not</u> in the instructions?

   ....

c What is the plural of *foot*? ....

4 Listen to Track 46 again. Put the pictures in Activity 2 in order.

a [ ]   b [ ]   c [1]   d [ ]   e [ ]

5 Listen to Track 46 again. Complete the instructions with the word you hear.

a Stand up with your .... by your side.

b Don't .... to breathe.

c Go down onto your .... and stand on your knees with your arms by your side.

d Bring your arms up beside your body and start to .... your chest.

e .... go too fast.

f Now take your left hand behind you and .... your left foot.

g Now put your right .... behind you and hold your right foot.

h Put your .... back and open your throat.

6 Listen to Track 46 again. Tick the words the yoga teacher uses to make her students feel good.

a Good.   [ ]   e I like that!   [ ]
b Excellent.   [ ]   f That's right.   [ ]
c That's very good. [ ]   g Nice.   [ ]
d Very nice.   [ ]

●●●B Speaking Describing and drawing

1 Match the shape with the name.

| circle   corner   straight line   rectangle   square   triangle |

a ......rectangle...... ....

2 Complete the sentences about the shapes in Activity 1. For each sentence, use first the phrases in the box and then the words in Activity 1.

| in the middle   at the top   at the bottom   in the top right-hand corner
in the bottom left-hand corner |

a There's a blue dot _at the top_ .... of _the triangle_ ....

b There's a pink dot .... of ....

c There's a red dot .... of ....

d There's a black dot .... of ....

e There's a green dot .... of ....

➡ Pronunciation Exercises A, Exercise 6

3 You want to give instructions to a friend to draw this picture. Write your instructions.

Example: Draw ... Put ... Make ... in the middle / at the top /
at the bottom / on the left / on the right

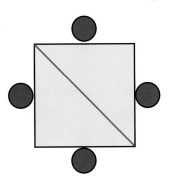

4 Describe and draw. Give your instructions to your friend. Complete the conversation.

TIM: OK. I'm ready for your instructions! Are they easy?

YOU: ....

TIM: A square or a rectangle? Big or small?

YOU: ....

TIM: OK, now what?

YOU: ....

TIM: Sorry. Can you say that again? Where do I draw the straight
line? In the middle?

YOU: ....

TIM: Oh, OK. A diagonal line then, from the top left-hand corner to the
bottom right-hand corner?

YOU: .... Now, ...

....

TIM: Four small circles, hmm, where?

YOU: ....

TIM: Are the circles touching the sides of the square?

YOU: ....

TIM: OK. Is that it? Look, is this OK?

YOU: ....

5 Listen to Track 47 and speak after the beep. Give your instructions.
Use your conversation in Activity 4.

●●●A Listening You and the weather

1 What's the weather like? Complete the sentences *a–e* with words from the box.

| snowing |
| raining |
| sunny |
| cloudy |
| windy |

a It's .... b It's .... c It's .... d It's .... e It's ....

2 You and the weather: how do you feel in these situations? Write sentences with the adjectives in the box.

a It's sunny.

........I feel happy........ .

b It's raining.

....

c It's snowing.

....

d It's windy.

....

e It's cloudy.

....

happy

sad

excited

bored

3 Look at the pictures. Answer the questions.

a What's the weather like at the zoo? ....windy........

b What's the weather like in town? ....

c What's the weather like at the park? ....

a [ ]   **b [ ]**   **c [ ]**

4 Listen to two people talking about the weather and activities on Track 48.
What do the people decide? Tick the correct picture in Activity 3, a, b or c.

5 Listen to Track 48 again. Mark the sentences True (T) or False (F).

a The weather at Maggie's place is sunny today.   [T]

b It is raining at Leo's place.   [   ]

c It is windy and it is raining at the zoo.   [   ]

d Maggie wants to go to the cinema.   [   ]

e The film at the cinema is about rain.   [   ]

f Leo likes zoos.   [   ]

6 Listen to Track 48 carefully again and complete these sentences from the conversation.

a Do you want to come to the zoo with us .... ?

b Well, it was awful .... , but today it's fine.

c Yesterday it was sunny all day here, but not .... !

d But it's .... here. It's just a little bit .... and a bit .... ,
but there's no .... at all.

e Are there any good .... on?

f I hear that .... is good.

g Let's go for a .... I don't like ....

h I can be at your place in an ....

7 What do you like to do when it's ...

a hot?

....

b raining?

....

c cold?

....

Write sentences.

Example: When it's really hot I like to sit under a tree and eat ice cream.

●●●B Speaking What shall we do?

1 Number the activities *1–4* in order of preference.
Then label the activities with adjectives from the box.

> expensive/cheap   interesting/boring   great/awful   lovely/terrible

2 Listen to Track 49 carefully. Respond to your friend Fred's ideas for an activity. Write your responses.

Example: FRED: *Let's go to the museum!*

YOU: *I don't like museums. They're boring.*

a FRED: (*National Park*)

YOU: ....

b FRED: (*swimming*)

YOU: ....

c FRED: (*skating*)

YOU: ....

d FRED: (*Museum of Technology*)

YOU: ....

Now listen to Track 50 and speak after the beep. Use your responses.

3 Now you give your ideas. Write them in the spaces.

Example: *Let's go to ... Why don't we go ... ?*
Do you want to go to ... ?

a YOU: (*Museum of Technology*) ....

....

b YOU: (*skating*) ....

....

c YOU: (*the cinema*) ....

....

d YOU: (*the zoo*) ....

....

4 Listen to Track 51 and give your ideas after the beep.
Use your conversation in Activity 3.
Listen to your friend carefully. Which ideas does she like?

[ ] ....

[ ] ....

[ ] cheap ....

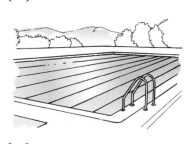

MUSEUM OF TECHNOLOGY

[ ] ....

●●A Listening Important past events

1 Match the dates and the historical events. Write the dates out in full.

> 12 October 1492   1876   3 April 1973   1951

a Columbus reached America. ...*The twelth of October fourteen ninety-two.*...

b The first colour TV programme in the USA. ....

c Alexander Graham Bell built the first telephone. ....

d Dr Martin Cooper invented the first mobile phone. ....

2 Listen to Track 52 and check your answers.

3 Which of these events is the most important: Man landing on the Moon, the invention of Concorde (a supersonic plane) or the invention of the Blackberry™?

a [   ]

b [   ]

c [   ]

4 Listen to Track 53, an interview in the street on 'the most important event in your lifetime'. Which picture is the man talking about?

5 Listen to Track 53 again. Are the sentences True (T) or False (F)?

a Man first landed on the Moon in 1969.   [T]

b The landing was on 16 July.   [   ]

c Three astronauts travelled in Apollo 11.   [   ]

d The three astronauts walked on the Moon.   [   ]

e Aldrin was the first man on the Moon.   [   ]

f People watched the Moon landing on television. [   ]

6 Read Armstrong's words. Choose the correct meaning.

'One small step for [a] man; one giant leap for mankind.'

(*Neil Armstrong, 20 July 1969, on the Moon*)

a Landing on the Moon was very important for the human race.   [ ]

b Landing on the Moon was very easy.   [ ]

c Landing on the Moon was very important for a man.   [ ]

7 Which inventions are important for your quality of life? Number the items in order of preference (1 = very important; 5 = not important).

a the car   [ ]

b the telephone   [ ]

c the computer   [ ]

d the DVD player   [ ]

e the cinema   [ ]

Now write sentences about your choices. Give reasons.

Example: The telephone is important for me because I like to keep in touch with people. The car isn't important, because I don't drive.

B Speaking Telling a story

➡ Pronunciation Exercises A, Exercises 26 and 27

1 Look at the story of Bonita Banana. Label the pictures with words from the box.

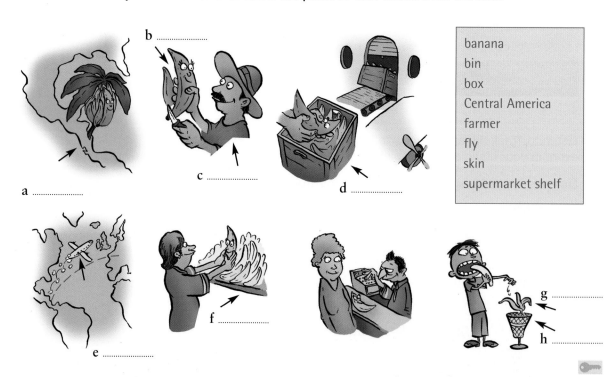

banana
bin
box
Central America
farmer
fly
skin
supermarket shelf

a ....

b ....

c ....

d ....

e ....

f ....

g ....

h ....

2 Tell the story of Bonita Banana. Use words from the table and words from Activity 1.

Useful verbs	Sequence markers
grew up picked (fruit) packed (in a box) flew (on a plane) put (on a supermarket shelf; in a bin) bought ate	First, Then, Next, After that, Finally,

Example: This is the story of Bonita Banana. Bonita grew up in ...

Check your story in the Answer Key, page 91.

3 Tell the story to Lisa. Complete the conversation.

YOU: Listen. I'm going to tell you the story of Bonita Banana .

LISA: Who is Bonita Banana?

YOU: ....

LISA: Where was she from?

YOU: ....

LISA: What happened to Bonita?

YOU: First a farmer ....

Then ....

LISA: Why did he put her in a box?

YOU: ....

LISA: All the way to England! What happened next?

YOU: ....

LISA: And what happened after that?

YOU: A woman .... and

a little boy ....

LISA: Poor Bonita Banana!

4 Listen to Track 54 and speak after the beep. Use your conversation in Activity 3.

●●●A Listening A day in London

1 Tick (✓) the places that are in London.

a Big Ben   [✓]   e Tower Bridge   [   ]

b Kew Gardens   [   ]   f The Empire State Building   [   ]

c Madame Tussaud's Wax Museum [   ]   g Brooklyn Bridge   [   ]

d Central Park   [   ]   h Buckingham Palace   [   ]

In which city are the three places that are not in London? ....

2 Find the following things in the three flyers.

a the name of three underground stations

1 <u>Kew Gardens</u>

2 ....

3 ....

b an expression that means 'the times when the place opens
and closes'

....

c an expression that means 'what is on at the moment'

....

d a word that means 'how much it costs to go in'

....

Opening hours: 9.30 – ....

🚇 **Kew Gardens**

Special Events:
Tropical Flowers

Admission: ....

a

Opening hours: ....

🚇 **Tottenham Court Road**

Special Events:
China Yesterday and Today

Admission: ....

b

Opening hours: ....

🚇 **Covent Garden**

Special Events:
Routemaster rides

Admission: ....

c

3 Listen to Track 55 and match the flyer a, b or c to the place.

The British Museum   [ ]

The Transport Museum   [ ]

The Royal Botanic Gardens [ ]

4 Listen to Track 55 again. Complete the information in the flyers.

5 Which place is good for these people?

a Pat and Louisa love flowers. ....

b Lun is from China. She doesn't like museums but she wants to see London from the top of a bus. ....

c John is interested in history. ....

●B Speaking Talking about a trip

1 Look at the pictures. Where can you do these activities?

a go surfing .... *Bondi Beach* ....

b go snorkelling ....

c see a modern building and listen to music ....

d go swimming ....

e climb a mountain ....

f see a famous bridge from a boat ....

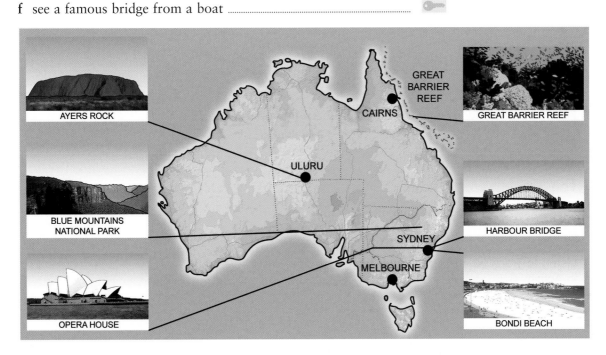

AYERS ROCK

GREAT BARRIER REEF

CAIRNS

GREAT BARRIER REEF

ULURU

BLUE MOUNTAINS NATIONAL PARK

HARBOUR BRIDGE

SYDNEY

MELBOURNE

OPERA HOUSE

BONDI BEACH

Look at the map. Which of the activities can you do in and around Sydney?

....

2 You went to Australia for your holiday. You went to Sydney and another place of your choice. Complete the information in the table.

Where did you go?	What did you do?	Did you like it?
In and around Sydney:		
In the other place (............................):		

3 Talk to Bruce, an Australian, about your holiday. Complete the conversation.

BRUCE: Where did you go for your holiday?

YOU: I went to Australia .

BRUCE: Really? I'm from Australia! Where did you go?

YOU: ....

BRUCE: I love Sydney. What do you think of the Opera House?

YOU: ....

BRUCE: Did you go to Bondi Beach?

YOU: ....

BRUCE: What about the Harbour Bridge? They have fantastic fireworks on New Year's Eve. Did you see that?

YOU: ....

BRUCE: Where else did you go?

YOU: ....

BRUCE: Really? I don't know that place. What did you do there?

YOU: ....

BRUCE: Did you like it?

YOU: ....

BRUCE: What was the best thing in Australia?

YOU: ....

4 Listen to Track 56 and speak after the beep. Use your conversation in Activity 3.

•●A Listening Plans and intentions

1 Tick (✓) the correct answer.

a What are the people in the picture celebrating?

They finished school.   [ ] ....

They graduated from university. [ ] ...P....

They started university.   [ ] ....

b How are the people in the picture feeling? (You can choose more than one answer.)

sad [ ] ....   happy [ ] ....   excited [ ] ....   nervous [ ] ....   frightened [ ] ....

c What are they going to do next?

They're going to get a job.   [ ] ....

They're going to see the world. [ ] ....

They're going to study more.   [ ] ....

2 Listen to Track 57. Which of your answers in Activity 1 are true of Peter and Chloe? Write P or C on the lines next to the answers.

3 Listen to Track 57 again. Who says these sentences, Chloe or Peter?

a 'Now we take a long, long holiday.'   ......Peter......

b 'I'm going to travel and see the world.'   ....

c 'Don't you want to get a good job?'   ....

d 'No, that can wait.'   ....

e 'I'm going to earn a lot of money.'   ....

f 'See you in Copacabana!'   ....

4 Listen to Track 57 again. Underline the words you hear.

PETER: No, that _can_ / _can't_ wait.

CHLOE: Hmm. I _think_ / _don't think_ so. I'm going to write to _some_ / _lots of_ companies and I'm _not going to_ / _going to_ work very hard. I'm going to earn _a lot of_ / _a little_ money. And then I'm going to travel. On holiday, you know.

PETER: _Great_ / _Bad_ plans! Meet me on Copacabana beach. You _can_ / _can't_ buy your poor friend a drink!

Chloe agrees to meet Peter on the beach. What does she say?

....

➡ Pronunciation Exercises A, Exercises 32 and 33

•••B Speaking Planning a party

1 You work as a party planner and you are organising a graduation party for 40 people. Choose the things you would like to have for the party and work out the cost. You've got £1,000 to spend.

Top band (£100 per hour)	✓	4 hours = £400
Best DJ in town (£70 per hour)		
Ballroom (£250 per night)		
Chic tables (£20 per table for 8)		
Hot dinners (menus from £15 per person)		
Finger food – original snacks (£5 per person)		
Party decorations (£150)		
University garden (£100 per night)		
Prizes for competitions (£50)		
Soft drinks (£4 per person)		
Cocktails (£10 per person)		
Total		

Write a list of your plans. Use verbs from the box.

| ask   get   have   hire   organise   serve   spend |

Example: I'm going to spend £400 on a good band. I'm not going to have expensive food.

....

....

....

....

2 Talk to your clients, Roberta and Ned, about your plans. Complete the conversation.

ROBERTA: I'd really like to hear about your plans!

NED: Yes, tell us about your plans. Where are you going to have the party?

YOU: _I'm going to_ ....

ROBERTA: How lovely! But how much is that going to cost?

YOU: ....

NED: That's OK, I guess. What about music?

YOU: ....

NED: Isn't that going to be expensive?

YOU: ....

ROBERTA: That sounds great! Is there going to be any food?

YOU: ....

ROBERTA: I'm not too sure about that. Are people going to sit down at tables?

YOU: ....

NED: What are people going to drink?

YOU: ....

ROBERTA: Well, everything sounds just fine. But what's going to make this party special? And how much are we going to spend in total?

YOU: ....

NED: Oh, I'm sure it's going to be a fantastic party. Thank you for all your work!

3 Listen to Track 58 and speak after the beep. Use your conversation in Activity 2.

4 It is the day after the graduation party you organised. A friend phones you to ask how it was. Listen to your friend on Track 59. Write your answers to the questions.

a QUESTION: How are you feeling after the party?

YOU: _Fine but very tired._ ....

b QUESTION:

YOU: ....

c QUESTION:

YOU: ....

d QUESTION:

YOU: ....

e QUESTION:

YOU: ....

5 Listen to Track 59 again and answer the questions after the beep.

●●●A Listening A radio play

1 Listen to the start of three radio plays on Track 60. Which play is a comedy, which play is a horror story and which play is a thriller?
Write the correct word in the table.

Play A	Play B	Play C

2 Listen to Track 60 again. Write some words for each play that helped you guess the answers.

A: ....

B: ....

C: ....

You are going to listen to a radio play called *Love is Blind*.
What's the play going to be like? Choose adjectives.

romantic [ ]   funny [ ]   dramatic [ ]   tragic [ ]   silly [ ]

3 Now listen to part of the play on Track 61*. Check your answers.

4 Listen to Kate and Lorna talking on Track 61 again. Are the sentences True (T) or False (F)?

Lorna   Max   Kim   Kate

a Kate and Lorna are friends.   [   ]

b Kate is getting married.   [   ]

c Kim and Lorna are best friends.   [   ]

d Max is Lorna's boyfriend.   [   ]

e Kim is going to have a birthday party.   [   ]

f Kate knows the name of Kim's boyfriend.   [   ]

*Tracks 61–114 are on CD 2.

5 What's going to happen next? Choose an ending.

   a Max and Lorna are going to get back together again.   [ ]

   b Kim is going to speak to Lorna and invite her to her party.   [ ]

   c Max is going to tell Kate that he loves her.   [ ]

   d Kate is going to tell Max that Lorna still loves him.   [ ]

   e We are going to find out who Kim is going to marry.   [ ]

Listen to Track 62 to check your answer.

6 Listen to Track 62 again. Write the words you hear.

KIM: Well, Max, did you (**a**) .... *speak* ..... to Lorna?

MAX: Well, I (**b**) .... her …

KIM: Yes, but when are you going to (**c**) .... her?

MAX: Next (**d**) .... , Kim. I promise. It's (**e**) .... , you know.

KIM: Oh Max! You must tell her soon. We're getting (**f**) .... next (**g**) .... !

MAX: I know, I know. Next week, I promise.

7 Read the summary of the story from a radio guide. Is it the same or different from the scene on Track 62?

> **6.15** *Love is Blind*. Max is angry with Kim.
> Max wants to tell Lorna that he is getting
> married. Kim doesn't want her to know until
> after the wedding. Max talks to Lorna tonight.

....

➡ Pronunciation Exercises C, Exercises 5–7

●●●B Speaking Breaking up is hard to do

1 Match the beginnings and the endings of these sentences.

Beginnings	Endings
a I feel sorry …	**1** I'm going to get married.
b Please don't …	**2** for Caroline.
c I don't know how to say this but …	**3** be friends.
d You're going to marry …	**4** I made you sad.
e I hope we can …	**5** get angry.
f I'm sorry …	**6** my best friend, aren't you?

2 Use the sentences in Activity 1 to respond to the people on Track 57. Complete the responses.

   a MAN: Do you feel sorry for me?

      YOU: _I feel sorry for Caroline_ .

   b MAN: What are you trying to say to me?

      YOU: _____ .

   c MAN: You are not going to like this: I'm getting married.

      YOU: _____ .

   d MAN: So you're not going out with Alex anymore?

      YOU: No, but _____ .

   e MAN: Oh, how can you do this to me? I feel so sad!

      YOU: _____ .

   f MAN: You broke my Blackberry™? That's so stupid! Aaargh!

      YOU: _____ .

Now listen to Track 63 and speak after the beep. Use your responses above.

3 Max finally tells Lorna his news. Write the scene. Then listen to Track 64 to compare your scene.

MAX: I don't know how to say this, Lorna,
     but … I'm getting married.

LORNA: _____

_____

_____

_____

_____

A Listening A radio game

1 Do you have radio or television game shows in your country? Do you watch them?
Match the words about game shows and their definitions.

Words about game shows	Definitions
1 presenter	**a** a nice thing people get when they win a game or a competition
2 contestant	**b** a person answering questions in a competition or game show
3 audience	**c** a person introducing a television or radio show
4 prize	**d** one stage or part of a game or competition
5 round (in a game)	**e** the best, most successful contestant in a game
6 winner	**f** a group of people in a television or radio studio, watching a game and applauding

2 Listen to Track 65. Are the sentences True (T) or False (F)?

a The name of the game is *The Price is Right*.　　　　[F]

b There are two contestants.　　　　[ ]

c The contestants have to guess the price of three
things in each round.　　　　[ ]

d The contestant who guesses the price, or comes near,
wins the round.　　　　[ ]

e The winner of the rounds can win a big prize.　　　　[ ]

3 Listen to Track 65 again. Play the game. Write the prices on the price tags.
Use the clues to help you.

Clues:
* Beatles collection: £50–£110. The records are more expensive than the CDs.

　• £　　　　　• £

* Guitars: £150–£400. The electric guitar is more
expensive than the Spanish guitar.

　• £　　　　　• £

* Sofas: £100–£1,500. One is real leather.

　• £　　　　　• £

* Car: price is higher than £10,000, lower than £16,000.

　• £

4 Listen to Track 66. Check the prices. Did you get the prices right? Did you win the car?

●●●B Speaking For sale

➠ Pronunciation Exercises B, Exercises 10 and 11

1 You want to sell some items. You put these ads in the newspaper.

Sony television, flat screen, 1 year old, under guarantee. Only ....
Brand new Panasonic DVD recorder. ....
Bargain! large fridge with small freezer. .... ono
Selling kitchen table with chairs – painted wood, perfect condition. ....

Answer the questions.

Which of the items ...

a are you prepared to sell for a little less money than the price you want?
the fridge (ono = or nearest offer)

b is made of wood? ....

c did you buy new but you never used? ....

....

d can be repaired by the manufacturer for free? ....

....

Now put a price on the items. Write the prices in the ads.

2 People are interested in your items. Listen to Track 67. Answer the phone calls and complete the conversations.

Phone call 1

MAN: Hello. I am interested in the DVD recorder you're selling ...

(*age*) .... ?

YOU: ....

MAN: (*guarantee*) .... ?

YOU: ....

MAN: Great! When can I come and see it?

YOU: ....

Phone call 2

WOMAN: Hi. I saw your ad in the paper. I'm interested in your kitchen table …

(*number of chairs*) .... ?

YOU: ....

WOMAN: (*colour*) .... ?

YOU: ....

WOMAN: (*price*) .... ?

YOU: ....

WOMAN: Thanks. I'll think about it.

Phone call 3

MAN: Hi! I'm phoning about the fridge.

(*brand*) .... ?

YOU: ....

MAN: (*colour*) .... ?

YOU: ....

MAN: (*price*) .... ?

YOU: ....

MAN: I can't pay that much. Can you take a little less?
What's your best price?

YOU: ....

MAN: Fair enough. When can I see the fridge?

(*address*) .... ?

YOU: ....

MAN: Great! See you then.

3 Listen to Track 67 again and speak after the beep. Use your conversations in Activity 2.

4 A friend phones you to ask you about the things you wanted to sell. Listen to Track 68.
Write answers for the questions.

a YOUR FRIEND: Hi! I wanted to ask you about the things you wanted to sell. Did you sell everything?

YOU: ....

b YOUR FRIEND: You didn't sell the DVD recorder? Oh good! How much do you want for it?

YOU: ....

c YOUR FRIEND: Wow! That's a lot. Can you give me a special price?

YOU: ....

d YOUR FRIEND: Thank you. That's nice of you. How old is the recorder?

YOU: ....

e YOUR FRIEND: That's great! Can I give you a cheque?

YOU: ....

f YOUR FRIEND: OK. I can come and collect it tomorrow. See you then!

5 Listen to Track 68 again and answer the questions after the beep.

●●●A Listening Giving advice

1 A member of your family gets a new, hi-tech DVD recorder for the first time. Tick (✓) the things you think may be a problem for the person.

a He/She doesn't understand the instructions. [ ]

b He/She can't use the remote. [ ]

c He/She is scared of all the buttons. [ ]

d He/She doesn't know how to record. [ ]

e He/She hates gadgets. [ ]

Now give the person advice. Use the ideas in the box.

> Read the instructions slowly and carefully again.
> Ask a member of your family to help.
> Calm down.
> Look at the pictures in the instructions.
> Get a simpler machine!
> Play with the different buttons and see what happens.
> Pay a technician.
> Ask the people at the shop to explain.

1 – Help! I can't understand the instructions!

YOU: *Why don't you read them again? / Read them again slowly and carefully.*

2 – I just can't use the remote!

YOU: ....

....

3 – Aargh. Look at all these buttons!

YOU: ....

....

4 – How do you record on this thing?

YOU: ....

....

5 – I hate these gadgets. They're too difficult!

YOU: ....

....

2 Listen to Track 69. Christina's mother has got a new DVD recorder. Number the parts of the remote as you hear them.

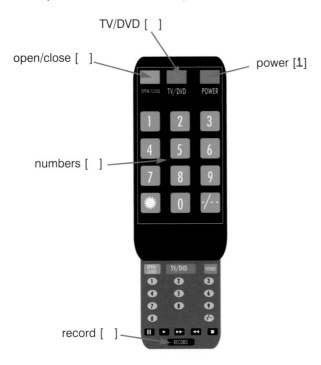

TV/DVD [ ]

open/close [ ]

power [1]

numbers [ ]

record [ ]

3 Listen to Track 69 again. Are the sentences True (T) or False (F)?

a Christina likes her mother's new DVD recorder.   [T]

b Christina's mother is following the instructions in the manual.   [ ]

c Christina's mother knows which is the power button.   [ ]

d You can get a picture every time you press the power button.   [ ]

e To choose channel 80, you press 8 + 0.   [ ]

f There is no record button.   [ ]

g Christina is good at following instructions.   [ ]

4 Listen to part of Track 69 again. Complete the script with the words you hear.

CHRISTINA: Wow, Mum! Is that your new DVD (a) ....? It's great!

MUM: Yes, but I can't use the (b) .... There are all these buttons!

CHRISTINA: Let me see. OK, to (c) .... it .... press this button

here at the (d) .... The one on the right.

MUM: I did that but nothing shows on the (e) ....

CHRISTINA: Ah, I know. You see this (f) .... in the middle here?

That's to (g) .... if you want television or DVD.

Check your answers in the audioscript on pages 83–84.

●●●B Speaking Giving an interview

1 You are the English Learner of the Year! Prepare for an interview for *Just Right Magazine*. Answer the questions in the table. Look at the model answers to help you.

Questions	Model answers	Your answers
What was your best experience as a learner of English this year?	I went to England. I tried speaking English and people understood me!	I ...
What was your most embarrassing experience as a learner of English?	I tried to help a tourist in my town and I couldn't give him good directions.	
What's your favourite time of day to study English?	Early morning, when it's quiet and I can concentrate.	
Why are you using a Listening and Speaking book at the moment?	I am practising my listening. and learning to communicate better.	
What is the best piece of technology to help you learn English more easily?	I like using a computer and reading things in English on the Internet.	
What are your plans and ambitions as a learner?	I'm going to continue learning English and I'm going to speak like a British person.	

2 Listen to Track 70. Listen to the interviewer's questions and speak after the beep. Use your answers in Activity 1.

•A Sounds

The alphabet

1 Listen to Track 71. Number the vowels *a, e, i, o, u* in the order you hear them.

A [1]   E [ ]   I [ ]   O [ ]   U [ ]

2 Listen to Track 72. Number the letters of the alphabet in the order you hear them.

A [ ]   B [ ]   C [ ]   D [ ]   E [ ]   F [ ]   G [ ]   H [ ]   I [ ]

J [ ]   K [ ]   L [ ]   M [ ]   N [ ]   O [ ]   P [ ]   Q [ ]   R [ ]

S [ ]   T [ ]   U [1]   V [ ]   W [ ]   X [ ]   Y [ ]   Z [ ]

3 Now write the letters under the correct sound. Which letters have these sounds?

/eɪ/	/iː/	e/	/aɪ/	/əʊ/	/uː/	/ɑː/
A	B	F	I	O	Q	R

Listen to the alphabet in the correct order on Track 73. Repeat the letters.

/ə/

4 Listen to the pronunciation of *a/an* on Track 74.
They have the sound /ə/.

a Are you a doctor?
b I'm an accountant.
c He isn't an engineer.
d Marie's a student.
e Is she an architect?

> Just note
> The sound /ə/ is called a schwa.

Now listen to Track 74 again and repeat the sentences.

5 Write your job or occupation here and practise saying it.

I'm ....

/ð/ and /d/

6 Listen to Track 75. Write the words under the correct sound.

this that daughter these those father brother mother Freddy with bad read

/ð/	/d/
this	daughter

Practise saying the words.

Present simple endings /s/, /z/ and /ɪz/

7 Listen to ten verbs on Track 76. Number the verbs in the order you hear them.

watches [ ]   sleeps [1]   goes [ ]   plays [ ]

flies [ ]   does [ ]   works [ ]   relaxes [ ]

washes [ ]   meets [ ]

8 Listen to Track 76 again. Pay attention to the endings. Write the verbs under the correct sound.

/s/	/z/	/ɪz/
sleeps	goes	watches

Practise saying the verbs. Pay attention to the pronunciation of the endings.

/t/ and /θ/

9 Listen to these words on Track 77 and underline the /t/ sounds.

foot   tooth   throat   three   healthy

two   month

Listen to Track 77 again and circle the /θ/ sounds.

10 Say these sentences with the correct pronunciation of /t/ and /θ/.

a My throat hurts.
b I play football twice a month.
c I'm healthy.

11 Write two true sentences about you with at least four words from Exercise 9. Practise saying your sentences with the correct pronunciation.

....

....

....

....

/ŋ/

12 Listen to these words on Track 78. Repeat the words. They all have the sound /ŋ/.

think   drink   thanks   having   falling   driving

watching   song   singing   going

13 Practise reading the sentences. Look at the letters underlined. Use the sound /ŋ/.

a Thanks for singing that song.
b I'm watching him and I think he's falling!

Listen to Track 79 and repeat the sentences.

Contractions of verb be

14 Listen to two dialogues on Track 80. Number the contractions in the order you hear them.

I'm [ ]

you're [1]

he's [ ]

she's [ ]

it's [ ]

we're [ ]

they're [ ]

15 Listen to Track 80 again. Complete the dialogues and repeat them.

a

Oh good. (1) .... here.

Yes, (2) .... here but (3) .... there.

(5) .... ready. (6) .... ready and (7) .... ready. But now it's raining!

b

(4) .... ready?

/ʌ/ and /ɒ/

16 Listen to Track 81. Look at the letters underlined. Which two words have a different sound?

l<u>o</u>ve   m<u>o</u>ney   d<u>o</u>es   l<u>o</u>t   <u>o</u>n

17 Listen to Track 82. Write these words under the correct sound.

club   Hong Kong   but   London   wrong
touch   stop   doesn't   contact

/ʌ/	/ɒ/
love	on

Listen to Track 82 again and repeat the words.

/s/ or /z/

18 Listen to the plurals of these words on Track 83. Pay attention to the endings. Write these words under the correct sound.

bedroom   box   desk   eye   lamp   sister
sofa   table

/s/	/z/	/ɪz/
bedrooms		

19 Complete these rules with /s/ or /z/

a If the word ends in the sounds /p/, /t/, /k/, /f/, /θ/, the plural is ....

b If the word ends in the sounds /b/, /d/, /g/, /v/, /ð/, /m/, /n/, /ŋ/, /l/, /r/, the plural is

....

c What about the plural of *fridge*? ....

Find other plurals and write them under the correct sound in the table in Exercise 18.

/r/

20 Listen to these sentences on Track 84 and notice the pronunciation of *r* when the following word starts with a vowel. Circle the *r* where you hear it.

Is there a bank near here?
Are there any shops near here?
There is a post office near the supermarket.

21 Read these conversations and circle the sound /r/ when you hear it.

a - Is there a hospital in this town?
    - Yes, there is. It's near the car park.
b - Are there any supermarkets near here?
    - Yes, there are. There are two.
c - Where is the town hall?
    - There isn't a town hall here.

Listen to Track 85 and check your answers. Practise saying the conversations with the same pronunciation.

/kən/, /kæn/ and /kɑːnt/

22 Listen to the pronunciation of *can* and *can't* on Track 86 and write the correct phonetic symbol.

/æ/   /ɑː/   /ə/

a Can you play the piano? ....

b No, I can't. ....

c Yes, I can. ....

Complete these rules. Write the phonetics.

1 If *can* is stressed, the pronunciation is
    ..../kæn/.......... .

2 When *can* is unstressed, the pronunciation is
    ....

3 *Can't* is pronounced ....

23 Read the conversation. What's the correct pronunciation of *can* and *can't*? Write the phonetics in the spaces.

MARIA: Can [..../kən/.....] you speak French?

JAMIE: No, I can't [.................]. I can [.................]

speak Dutch and German, but I can't

[.................] speak French. Can [.................]

you?

MARIA: Yes, I can [.................].

Now listen to Track 87 and check your answers. Practise reading the dialogue.

/aɪ/ and /aʊ/

24 Listen to these words on Track 88 and write the correct sound, /aɪ/ or /aʊ/ next to the word.

a mouse ....

b rhino ....

25 Listen to these sentences on Track 89. Underline the /aʊ/ sounds and circle the /aɪ/ sounds.

a Look out for the mouse.
b That's too loud now. Turn it down.
c Mind the wild animal.
d Find the white dog.
e There's a mouse in the house.
f Put your right hand behind you.

Practise saying the sentences.
Write two more words you know that have each of these sounds.

Pronunciation of -*ed* endings: /d/, /t/ and /ɪd/

26 Listen to these verbs on Track 90. Pay attention to the -*ed* endings. Write the verbs under the correct sound.

died ended finished jumped kissed landed
lifted lived played studied wanted watched
worked

/d/	/t/	/ɪd/
died	finished	landed

Practise saying the verbs with the correct pronunciation.

27 Read the groups of verbs aloud. Cross out the verb with a different pronunciation of -*ed*.

a played   turned   lived   ~~liked~~
b kissed   cooked   died   watched
c wanted   beheaded   washed   decided
d arrived   reached   loved   divorced
e landed   ended   lifted   happened
f started   worked   baked   walked

Listen to Track 91 to check your answers.

/eɪ/ and /e/

28 Write the words under the correct sound.

later letter let late tale tell pepper
paper wait wet

/eɪ/	/e/
eight	bed

Listen to Track 92 to check your answers, then repeat the words.

29 Practise saying these sentences.

   a Wait. The paint is wet.
   b Is there any paper for the letter?
   c Write the letter later.

For each of the sounds, add three words you know to the table.

/iː/ and /ɪ/

30 Listen to Track 93. Which word do you hear first? Number the words in each pair 1 or 2 as you hear them.

/iː/			/ɪ/		
wheel	[ ]		will	[1]	
eat	[ ]		it	[ ]	
least	[ ]		list	[ ]	
team	[ ]		Tim	[ ]	
feel	[ ]		fill	[ ]	

Repeat the pairs.

What spellings are often pronounced with the sound /iː/?

31 Write the words underlined under the correct sound in the table in Exercise 30.

   a <u>Sit</u> down and eat your <u>meat</u>.
   b <u>Please</u> take a <u>seat</u>, <u>Phil</u>.
   c Tim's team is going to <u>win</u>.
   d <u>Listen</u> and fill <u>in</u> the blanks on your <u>sheet</u>.
   e <u>This</u> <u>machine</u>'s very <u>quick</u>.

Listen to Track 94 to check your answers. Practise reading the sentences aloud.

/tuː/ and /tə/ (going to)

32 Listen to Track 95. Choose the correct pronunciation of *to*, /uː/ as in *food* or /ə/ as in *the*.

   a Are you going to /tuː/ /tə/ ask her to /tuː/ /tə/ come?
   b I'm going to /tuː/ /tə/ tell you a secret.
   c How's it going to /tuː/ /tə/ end?
   d They're going to /tuː/ /tə/ have a party.

Which sound goes before a vowel? Read out the sentences.

33 Choose the correct pronunciation. Practise saying the sentences aloud.

   a I'm going to /tuː/ /tə/ ask you a question and you're going to /tuː/ /tə/ answer.
   b You're going to /tuː/ /tə/ talk and I'm going to /tuː/ /tə/ listen.
   c I'm going to /tuː/ /tə/ open the door. Are you going to /tuː/ /tə/ come in?

Listen to Track 96 to check your answers.

/e/, /æ/, /ʌ/ and /ɜː/

34 Listen to Track 97. Repeat the words with the sound /ɜː/.

   burn   world   turn   bird   girl

35 Listen to Track 98. Write the words under the correct sound.

   ten   tan   tonne   turn   pan   pen   pun   Dad
   dead   cat   cut   Kurt   cup   cap

/e/	/æ/	/ʌ/	/ɜː/
bed	bad	bud	bird
Ben	ban	bun	burn

Practise saying the words: read down the columns first, then across.

36 Listen to Track 99. Repeat these sentences aloud. Add the words underlined to the table in Exercise 35.

   a I <u>plan</u> to <u>marry</u> <u>Jerry</u>.
   b I <u>heard</u> it <u>had</u> two <u>heads</u>!
   c Ben <u>burnt</u> the buns.

●●●B Stress

Word stress (countries and nationality words)

1 Listen to Track 100 and underline the stressed syllable.

a Bra<u>zil</u>	Brazilian
b Canada	Canadian
c Russia	Russian
d Japan	Japanese
e China	Chinese
f Korea	Korean
g Mexico	Mexican
h Australia	Australian
i South Africa	South African

2 Practise saying the words in the same way.

3 Say the nationality words. Match them according to their stress (first or second syllable).

Mexican   Korean   Australian   Brazilian
British   (South) African   Canadian   Russian

Mexican	Korean

What nationalities in Exercise 1 have a different stress from the name of the country?

Canadian – Canada, ...

Sentence stress

4 Listen to Track 101 and underline the word that has the main stress.

a How much is this <u>dress</u>?
b How much are those shoes?
c How much does it cost?
d How much are the apples?
e How much is that cheese?
f How many do you want?

Practise saying the sentences with the correct stress.

5 Underline the word that has the main stress in these questions.

a How many <u>apples</u> do you want?
b How much bread do you want?
c How many eggs do you want?
d How much salad do you want?
e How much does this meat cost?
f How many bananas do you want?

Now listen to Track 102 and check your answers.

6 Listen to Track 103. Underline the stressed word.

a How much is that shirt?
b Can you speak slowly, please?
c She's got dark brown hair.
d He's got light blue eyes.
e Can I take a message?
f How much does it cost?

Practise saying the questions with the correct pronunciation.

7 Listen to these sentences on Track 104. Which part of the verb *have to* is stressed?

a I don't have to go.
b I have to go.

8 Practise saying these sentences with the correct pronunciation of *have to*.

a We have to prepare for the test.
b They don't have to get up early.
c She has to send emails.
d He doesn't have to speak French at work.

Listen to Track 105 and check your answers.

9 Listen to Track 106 and number the sentences in the order you hear them.

a I have to wait in the gym.   [1]
   I have two weights in the gym.   [2]
b They don't have to play in the theatre.   [   ]
   They don't have two plays in the theatre. [   ]
c She has to work in the museum.   [   ]
   She has two works in the museum.   [   ]

Underline the stressed words. Practise saying the sentences with the correct stress and pronunciation.

10 Listen to Track 107. Underline the words that are stressed.

    a Sue's taller than John.
    b John's older than Sue.
    c This book's shorter than that one.
    d She's nicer than he is.

How is *than* pronounced, /ðən/ or /ðæn/? Write three more comparative sentences. Practise reading them aloud.

11 Read the sentences. Underline the words that are stressed in each sentence.

    a Beaches are hotter than mountains.
    b This book's more interesting than that one.
    c Bob's shorter than Peter.
    d He's more attractive than Peter.
    e Miranda's as clever as Tim.
    f Today's better than yesterday and not as good as tomorrow.

Listen to Track 108 to check your answers.

Now complete the rule.

In comparative sentences we usually stress the important words: the ......*comparative adjective*...... and the things we are comparing. Contractions and the words .... , ... , ... , and .... are not usually stressed.

••• C Intonation

Intonation in *yes/no* questions

1 Listen to Track 109. Does the voice go up or down at the end? Mark the questions ↗ (up) or ↘ (down).

a Are you married? ↗
b Are you a teacher?
c Are you English?
d Do you like chocolate?
e Does your friend eat snacks?

2 Listen to Track 109 again. Repeat the questions.

Intonation in questions

3 Listen to these questions on Track 110. Listen to the intonation.

Is the intonation in the second sentence the same (S) or different (D)?

a What's your name?
   Where do you live?   [S]

b Do you like playing football?
   Does he live in France?   [ ]

c When does she go shopping?
   Does she go shopping on Fridays? [ ]

d Do they like travelling?
   When do they travel?   [ ]

4 Read these sentences. Does the intonation go up or down? Mark the sentences ↗ (up) or ↘ (down).

a What's your name? ↘
b Do you live here?
c Where do you live?
d When do you go shopping?
e Do you like travelling?
f Does he work in a bank?

Now listen to Track 111 and check your answers.

Intonation: expressing feelings

5 Listen to Track 112 and repeat the sentences.

a That's awful!
   That's great!

b I hate shopping.
   I love shopping.

c I'm very tired.
   I'm very happy.

d It's too cold.
   It's too hot.

Practise saying the sentences with the same stress and intonation.

6 Listen to Track 113. Decide whether these people are happy (H) or sad (S).

a [ ]   b [ ]   c [ ]   d [ ]   e [ ]   f [ ]

7 Can you guess what the people are saying? Write sentences.

a ....
b ....
c ....
d ....
e ....
f ....

Listen to Track 114 and check your answers.

AUDIOSCRIPTS

CD 1

Track 1

1 CLAUDIO: Hello. My name's Claudio.
CECILIA: I'm Cecilia. Nice to meet you, Claudio.
2 CECILIA: Hi. I'm Cecilia. What's your name?
FRANK: I'm Frank, Frank Lewis. How are you?
3 CECILIA: Claudio, this is Frank.
CLAUDIO: Hello Frank. Pleased to meet you.
FRANK: Nice to meet you too.
4 FRANK: Paula, this is Cecilia. And this is Claudio.
PAULA: Nice to meet you both.
CLAUDIO: Hi Paula. How are you?
PAULA: Not bad, thank you.

Track 2

JO: Hi! I'm Jo. What's your name?
JO: Nice to meet you too.

Track 3

HELENA: Hello. I'm Helena. What's your name?
HELENA: Nice to meet you.
HELENA: This is my friend Marco.
MARCO: Hi. How are you?

Track 4

1 JIMMY: Good morning, Miss Brown.
MISS BROWN: Hello, Jimmy.
JIMMY: How are you?
MISS BROWN: Very well, thanks.
2 MR JONES: Good afternoon.
RECEPTIONIST: Good afternoon, Mr Jones.
MR JONES: How are you?
RECEPTIONIST: I'm very well, thank you. And you?
MR JONES: Fine, thank you.
3 DOORMAN: Good evening.
WOMAN: Hello.
DOORMAN: How are you?
WOMAN: Fine, thank you.
4 MAN: Hello Marty.
MARTY: Hi!
MAN: How's it going?
MARTY: Not bad, thanks. You?
MAN: Fine, thanks.
5 DIRAN: Hi Judy!
JUDY: Hi Diran!
DIRAN: How's it going?
JUDY: Fine, thanks.

Track 5

a CAROLINE: Good morning, Alison.
ALISON: Hi Caroline. How are you?
CAROLINE: Not bad, thanks. You?

b MR JOHNSON: Good afternoon.
MR BROOK: Good afternoon, Mr Johnson.
MR JOHNSON: How are you?
MR BROOK: I'm very well, thank you. And you?
c MEGAN: Good evening, Mrs Loder.
MRS LODER: Hello Megan.
MEGAN: How are you?
MRS LODER: Very well, thanks.
d LUCY: Hello Jimmy!
JIMMY: Hi Lucy! How's it going?
LUCY: Fine, thanks.

Track 6

MARIE: Hello. I'm Marie.
MARIE: Guess!
MARIE: No, I'm not French.
MARIE: That's right!

Track 7

oh/zero, one, two, three, four, five, six, seven, eight, nine, ten, eleven, twelve, thirteen, fourteen, fifteen, sixteen, seventeen, eighteen, nineteen, twenty

Track 8

ten, five, fifteen, zero, two, sixteen, twenty, eleven, fourteen, three, one, nine, nineteen, seven, seventeen, twelve, eight, eighteen, four, six, thirteen

Track 9

a WOMAN1: What's your phone number?
WOMAN 2: It's 0208 495 3497.
WOMAN1: Great. I'll call you.
b MAN: What's your telephone number, Lil?
LIL: 0703 034856.
MAN: I'll talk to you tomorrow then.
c WOMAN: What's your phone number, sir?
MAN: 0178 82545.
WOMAN: Thank you.
d MAN: What's your phone number, Jake?
JAKE: 07882 945 620.
MAN: Thank you very much.

Track 10

a MAN: What's your email address, Maria?
MARIA: marilou@yahoo.com
b WOMAN 1: Do you have email, Mary?
MARY: Yes, it's mari_lou@yahoo.co.uk

Track 11

RECEPTIONIST: The Just Right School of English. Good morning.
MARIA: I'd like some information about your school.
RECEPTIONIST: Sure. What's your name?
MARIA: Maria Lozano.

RECEPTIONIST: How do you spell your last name?

MARIA: L–O–Z–A–N–O.

RECEPTIONIST: Thanks. Where are you from, Maria?

MARIA: I'm Spanish.

RECEPTIONIST: Do you have email?

MARIA: Yes.

RECEPTIONIST: Good. What's your email address?

MARIA: mariloz@yahoo.com

RECEPTIONIST: Sorry? Mari-what?

MARIA: Mariloz.

RECEPTIONIST: How do you spell that?

MARIA: M–A–R–I–L–O–Z.

RECEPTIONIST: Great. And your phone number?

MARIA: 0207 857 2496.

RECEPTIONIST: Thanks. I'll send you the information immediately.

MARIA: Thanks. Bye.

Track 12

RECEPTIONIST: Hello, the Just Right School of English!

CLAIRE: Can you give me some information please?

CLAIRE: Claire Baudson.

CLAIRE: B–A–U–D–S–O–N.

CLAIRE: I'm French.

CLAIRE: c.baudson@mynet.co.uk

CLAIRE: 03850 09486. It's my mobile phone.

CLAIRE: Thanks. Bye.

Track 13

CAROLINE: This is really difficult! Who's this?

SHIRLEY: Picture a? Easy. It's Susan Lee.

CAROLINE: Really? Oh, OK. What about this baby in picture c?

SHIRLEY: And picture c is Joseph Smith. And picture f is Miriam.

CAROLINE: Are you sure?

SHIRLEY: Yeah, easy.

CAROLINE: OK. And who's the baby in picture d? Is it Zack?

SHIRLEY: Yes. Picture d Zack, e Olivia, and picture b Kenny. Easy.

Track 14

CAROLINE: This is really difficult! Who's this?

SHIRLEY: Picture a? Easy. It's Susan Lee.

CAROLINE: Really? Oh, OK. What about this baby in picture c?

SHIRLEY: And picture c is Joseph Smith. And picture f is Miriam.

CAROLINE: Are you sure?

SHIRLEY: Yeah, easy.

CAROLINE: OK. And who's the baby in picture d? Is it Zack?

SHIRLEY: Yes. Picture d Zack, e Olivia, and picture b Kenny. Easy.

CAROLINE: Let's check the answers. OK. Baby a is Susan, baby b is Zack. Baby c is Miriam, d is Kenny, e is Olivia and f is Joseph.

SHIRLEY: Oh!

CAROLINE: Oh, yeah, easy!

Track 15

JOAN: Hi. I'm Joan. What's your name?

JOAN: Where are you from?

JOAN: I'm from Manchester, England. Tell me what you look like. Is your hair short or long?

JOAN: My hair is dark and short. Is your hair dark too?

JOAN: My eyes are brown. What about your eyes? What colour are they?

JOAN: Send me a photo. Talk to you again soon. Bye!

Track 16

1 The train arriving at platform 2 is the 7.15 to London Waterloo, calling at Woking, Clapham Junction and London Waterloo. (repeated)

2 The train now at platform 6 is the 7.25 train to Southampton, calling at Winchester and Southampton. (repeated)

3 Passenger Julian Jones on Intercontinental Airlines flight 308 to Miami, please come to Gate 13A. Julian Jones, please come to Gate 13A, where flight IA308 to Miami is ready to depart.

4 Varig Airlines announces its flight VA407 to Rio de Janeiro, boarding at Gate 30A. Flight VA407 to Rio de Janeiro now boarding at Gate 30A.

5 British Airways flight BA601 to Mexico City is now boarding at Gate 10. Passengers on Flight BA601, please board at Gate 10.

Track 17

JO: Today is Monday. I hate Mondays! Do you like Mondays?

JO: What do you do on weekdays?

JO: What's your favourite day of the week?

JO: Why?

JO: My favourite day is Saturday. I go shopping and I meet my friends. I love Saturdays!

Track 18

1 WOMAN: Hola! Yo hablo español. Y tú?

MAN: You too can speak perfect Spanish! And French, and Japanese! The Language School is now open. Courses begin on 1st of September. Give us a call on 03978 596 3045 now!

2 Want to keep fit? Join Bodies Gym for a personalised exercise programme. Special January prices: £30 a month and a week's free trial. Join now! For more information call 95723 5936 or visit our website at www.bodiesgym.com.

3 What will you have tonight? Juicy hamburgers at £2.50 for six? Fresh chicken at £4.80 a kilo? How about sweet juicy Spanish oranges at only 50 pence a kilo? Or delicious chocolate cake with white chocolate icing, just £3.50? Where? At Food Mart, your local supermarket – fresh food at good prices. Hurry! Prices valid this week only.

Track 19

WOMAN: Hi!

WOMAN: Sure.

WOMAN: Snacks? Like crisps and sweets? Sure. I love snacks!

WOMAN: I don't eat hamburgers every day but I eat meat every day.

WOMAN: Eight glasses? I probably drink about 12, or more!

WOMAN: Well, I don't like fish so I never eat it.

WOMAN: I have a cup of tea in the morning but I don't drink coffee.

WOMAN: Mmm. Yes! I love ice cream, especially chocolate. So, do I eat well or badly?

Track 20

Welcome to the Odeon Cinema. Here are the films for this week.

On Screen One: *Small Adventures*, a film for all the family about Rachel Small and her family. Shows at 1.00 p.m., 3.00 p.m. and 5.00 p.m.

Screen One: *Terror in London*, for people over 18. Shows at 7.00 p.m. and 9.30 p.m.

Screen Two: *Always*, a romantic comedy for all ages, starring Tom Merton and Cristina Crawford. Shows at 3.30 p.m., 7.15 p.m. and 9.45 p.m.

Screen Three: *Today's Hero*, an action film starring Harry Murray. First at 3.30 p.m., then at 6.00 p.m. and at 8.30.

Thank you for calling the Odeon Cinema.

Track 21

JO: I'm ready to play. Ask your first question.

JO: I live in California.

JO: Yes, I do live in Hollywood.

JO: Yes, I do. I love films.

JO: My favourite film is *The Queen*. It's about the queen of England.

JO: A hobby? Yes, I collect autographs of famous film stars.

JO: Yes, I do. But I'm not an actor. I sell the tickets!

JO: That's right! My turn now. Here is my first question …

Track 22

NURSE 1: Dr Brown! We have an emergency in room 5.

DOCTOR: I'll be right there, Nurse.

JIMMY: My leg! Oooh … my leg hurts.

DOCTOR: Hello Jimmy. Your leg hurts? OK, let me see. Uh-huh. Does your foot hurt too?

JIMMY: Ow. Yes.

DOCTOR: Your leg is broken.

NURSE 1: Dr Brown! Michael James needs you in room 8. It's his head.

DOCTOR: I'll be right there, Nurse. Take care of Jimmy.

NURSE 1: Yes, doctor.

DOCTOR: Now Michael. What's the matter?

MICHAEL: My head hurts, doctor.

DOCTOR: Nurse, take Michael for an X-ray.

NURSE 2: Dr Brown! Room 3.

DOCTOR: What's the problem here?

NURSE 2: Her stomach hurts.

DOCTOR: Let me see. What's your name?

GIRL: Melanie. Oooh, it hurts.

DOCTOR: OK, Melanie. I want you to be a brave girl and take this medicine. OK?

GIRL: OK.

DOCTOR: Good girl.
Now I need to eat something. Do you like hamburgers, Nurse?

NURSE 2: Yes, doctor.

DOCTOR: Good! Me too. Let's go.

Track 23

DOCTOR: What's the matter?

DOCTOR: Tell me about your job. Do you have a lot of work?

DOCTOR: Do you use a computer at work?

DOCTOR: How often do you exercise?

DOCTOR: Do you eat a good breakfast?

DOCTOR: What do you do to relax?

DOCTOR: Hmm. I think you need to relax more often. You will feel better soon.

Track 24

You're listening to Hot Shop Radio – the best clothes at the best prices. Have you seen our hot new dresses? Only 19.99 in black and green and T-shirts at only 4.99 in sizes small, medium and large. In our shoe department, the latest summer styles in sandals at just 14.99.

For the guys, we have great casual shirts for just 9.99, small, medium, large and extra-large, and grey suits cost just 49.99. With prices like these, you can't afford to miss the bargains.

Now, let's play some music, it's back to the nineties with …

Track 25

a WOMAN: I want to take a mobile phone.
   MAN: Yes, that's a good idea.

b WOMAN: I want to spend more money. What do you think?
   MAN: Hmm. I'm not sure about that.

c WOMAN: How about a computer?
   MAN: No, that's not a good idea.

d WOMAN: Let's take some hamburgers.
   MAN: OK, that's fine.

e WOMAN: I want to buy an MP3 player.
   MAN: Oh yeah. Great!

f WOMAN: I want to take some sandals.
   MAN: Sandals! What a terrible idea!

Track 26

WOMAN: OK, what do you want to take for entertainment, for fun?

WOMAN: OK, that's fine. But I want to take lots of CDs too. What do you think?

WOMAN: OK. What about food?

WOMAN: Hmm. I'm not sure about that. What about clothes? I want to take my new dress.

WOMAN: All right. What about the money? How much is it for all that?

WOMAN: That's fine. But, it's very cold now. How about going camping in the summer when the weather is warm?

Track 27

SUE: It's a beautiful day for the carnival here at Notting Hill.

MAN: Yes, it is, Sue. A perfect day! The sun is shining, very hot...

SUE: Here comes the next band. Look at that! It's the children's Brixton group. They're wearing fantastic clothes, erm, costumes. Fabulous colours: yellow, red, green, black.

MAN: And listen to that music!

SUE: Yes, the band is playing calypso music. It's great music from the Caribbean. The children are dancing to the music, they're great dancers!

MAN: The public just love these children. Now everyone's clapping and dancing. Listen to that!

SUE: ... and here comes the next group. They're the Real Steel band. They're wearing...

Track 28

a Tom's riding a bike.
b Tina and Katie are playing baseball.
c Mia's walking.
d Alex is running.
e Nicky's playing the guitar.
f Anna's listening to Nicky.
g Sam's climbing a tree.
h Jill and Andy are dancing.

Track 29

LENNY: Have you got five young men, Alex, Sam, Nicky, Andy and Tom?

LENNY: Is Alex running?

LENNY: Is Tom lying on the grass?

LENNY: OK. That's one difference. What's Andy doing?

LENNY: He's driving a car in my picture. So that's two differences. Is Nicky listening to Anna? She's playing the guitar.

LENNY: Aha! Two more differences. What's Sam doing?

LENNY: Have you got five young women, Mia, Jill, Tina, Katie and Anna?

LENNY: What are they doing?

LENNY: So only Anna is different. How many differences do we have?

LENNY: Great! That was fun.

Track 30

LARS: Welcome to the School of Fashion Winter Show.

STEPHANIE: Thanks for coming. Let's get started. Here is Ella. Ella's wearing a green dress by Enzo Muriatti, and brown shoes – great winter clothes for young women.

LARS: Next is Marco, wearing a suit by Abel Schmitt. It's a pink suit and he is wearing it with a white T-shirt. What do you think about the colour, Stephanie?

STEPHANIE: I think it's great, but here comes Giulio. He's wearing black trousers and a sweater. Nice, but not very original. What do you think, Lars?

LARS: No, sweaters are not very original but they are great for men of all ages. Next is a suit by Anna Jacobs. Short trousers and a short jacket. What do you think, Stephanie?

STEPHANIE: Very elegant, and I love the shirt and tie. The next model is wearing …

Track 31

JAMIE: Lets play a game. You choose one of the people and I guess who it is, OK? How tall is the person?

JAMIE: What does the person look like?

JAMIE: What's he or she wearing?

JAMIE: Is it Monica?

JAMIE: OK. Your turn now. You ask the questions.

JAMIE: Very tall. About 1.80m, I think.

JAMIE: Well, tall and thin with short red curly hair.

JAMIE: Guess!

JAMIE: Yes, he's wearing a brown suit.

JAMIE: That's right!

Track 32

CATH: Hello?

TIM: Hi. Can I speak to Martha, please?

CATH: Sorry. She's not in the office at the moment. Can I take a message?

TIM: Yes. This is Tim Franklin. I'm sending her a fax for Mr Roberts. It's very important. The meeting with the manager is at 3.00, not at 4.00. And tell her to meet me at the restaurant at 8.00.

CATH: OK. Don't worry. I'll tell her.

Track 33

CATH: Hello?

MARTHA: Cath? It's Martha. Any messages?

CATH: Yes. Tim called. He's sending you a fax for the manager. You have a meeting with Mr Roberts at 4.00 and dinner with Frank at 8.00. It's very important!

MARTHA: Oh, OK. Thanks! Bye!

Track 34

INT: Hello? We are doing a survey about technology and communication. Can you answer some questions?

INT: Do you use a computer?

INT: What do you use your computer for?

INT: Do you send emails to friends and family or only for work?

INT: Do you ever write cards or letters?

INT: Right. What about your mobile phone? When do you use your mobile phone?

INT: One last question. Do you have a web page?

INT: Why?

INT: Well, that's it. Thank you very much for your help.

Track 35

1 A mobile phone has been found under a table at Friendy's Restaurant. Please come to the information desk to identify it.

2 If you have lost a green sweater, please come to the information desk. The sweater was found next to the supermarket.

3 We have a little lost child here. Her name is Melanie and she's about five years old. She has brown hair and brown eyes. Melanie's parents, please come and pick Melanie up. We found her in the toy store.

4 There is a lost dog in the shopping centre. Dogs are not permitted in the shopping centre. Please come and retrieve your dog. The dog is brown and is wearing a collar that says 'Matilda' and there is a telephone number. Matilda was found near the bank.

5 A woman's wallet has been found on the counter at Jim's bookstore. It contains a driving licence and credit cards. Please come and claim your wallet.

Track 36

a Have you got any sofas in your living room?

b What colour are your sofas?

c Have you got any chairs in the room?

d Have you got a coffee table in the room?

e Where is your coffee table?

f Are you happy with your new room?

g What's your favourite thing in the room?

Track 37

MAN: You've got a new house? How exciting! What's your new living room like?

MAN: Is there any furniture in the room?

MAN: Where is the big sofa?

MAN: And the small one? Where is the small sofa?

MAN: And where's the small table?

MAN: Where are the lamps?

MAN: Have you got rugs in the room?

MAN: Well, that sounds nice. Hey, what about the television? Where is the television?

MAN: No television? That's not possible. A house without a television is not a home!

Track 38

TOUR GUIDE: Welcome to the house of Marlene Murray, the world-famous actor. This is the living room. As you can see, it is beautiful – there is a sofa from France and the chairs are from Italy.

This is one of the bedrooms. There are 12 bedrooms in the house and ten bathrooms. This is Marlene's bedroom.

Down here is the kitchen – Marlene has ten cooks, but they don't all work at the same time.

There are two dining rooms. This is the one that Marlene uses every day and there is one dining room for special occasions.

There is no garden, but there is a swimming pool and a tennis court. Marlene opens the swimming pool twice a week to the local children, but today it is closed.

Well, I do hope you enjoyed your visit and that you will visit us again soon.

Track 39

LORNA: Where do you live?

LORNA: Is it a good place to live?

LORNA: Are there any places to go shopping?

LORNA: What about entertainment? Are there any places for that?

LORNA: Is it a good place for children?

LORNA: Is there anything special, like a large hospital or something?

LORNA: My town? Well, it's very beautiful but very, very small.

LORNA: A shopping centre? No, there isn't. There are only a few shops and there is no cinema!

LORNA: Yes, it is a good place to live… if you are 80 years old!

Track 40

a NEWSREADER: It's 9 o'clock. This is the World Today. The Prime Minister is on an official visit to France. He is meeting the French president in Paris and talking to French businessmen about …

b SPORTS COMMENTATOR: It was an exciting day in European football today. Here are the results. Manchester United 2, Barcelona 1; Liverpool 3, Chelsea 1; AC Milan 5, Real Madrid 3; Lyon 0, Bayern München 0 …

c WEATHERMAN: You are listening to Radio Capital. Come Rain or Shine! The weather in the capital today: it will be cloudy with showers and sunny intervals. Take your umbrella. Temperatures will reach 10°C so put on your coat! …

d PRESENTER: This is Theatre at Home. Sit down, relax and listen to today's play, *Who let the cat out?* by Joanna Firth. Maisie Lunn is played by Grace Ellis, Toby Grant plays Maurice.

MAISIE: Maurice? Maurice? Are you sleeping again?

MAURICE: No. I'm just thinking. What's the matter? You sound worried.

Track 41

SUSIE: ... so that was the Beatles with an old favourite. You're listening to Radio Barrowtown 95.4 FM. My name's Susie Martin and I'll be with you for the next two hours, playing the songs you want to hear for the people you love! I've had an email from Kevin March in Marlow (hello Kevin), and he says, 'Dear Susie, I love your show (thanks Kevin) and I'd like to hear a song for my lovely wife, Joanne, and our twin sons Jack and Brian. It's our tenth wedding anniversary on Tuesday the 2nd of April and it's my birthday on the 3rd of April (I can't tell you my age) and it's Jack and Brian's birthday on the 4th of April (they'll be four).' Wow! It sounds like a big party for you this weekend, Kevin. '... Can you play *Perfect Day* by Lou Reed for Joanne and the boys?' Of course I can, Kevin. This is Lou Reed with *Perfect Day* for Kevin March and his wife Joanne on their anniversary and for Jack and Brian March on their fourth birthday. Happy anniversary and happy birthday ...

Track 42

DJ: You are listening to YourTown Radio on 92.8 FM. Do you want us to play a special song for a special person? Phone now! ... And here's our first caller. Hello? Who's calling?

DJ: Where are you calling from?

DJ: What song do you want to hear?

DJ: Is this for a special person?

DJ: Is it for a special occasion?

DJ: What's your message?

DJ: Great! Any other song you want to play?

DJ: Who is it for?

DJ: Any message? What do you want to say?

DJ: That is lovely. Here are the songs – just for you.

Track 43

a What time do you get up?

b What time do you have lunch?

c What time do you go to bed?

d What time do you start work or go to school?

e What time do you finish working or studying?

f Do you like your routine?

Track 44

AUDREY: Hi Rob!

ROB: Oh hello.

AUDREY: What's the matter?

ROB: It's my new timetable for this term. It's awful.

AUDREY: What's wrong with it?

ROB: I have a class every day at 9 a.m.! I hate getting up early.

AUDREY: You poor thing! Do you have to go to every class?

ROB: Yes. Monday, Wednesday and Friday I have biology from 9.00 to 11.00 and on Tuesday and Thursday I have chemistry.

AUDREY: Oh well, does that mean you finish early every day?

ROB: No! I have to be in the lab every afternoon until 5.00!

AUDREY: Oh no! That's terrible!

ROB: I know! I have biology lab from 1.00 to 5.00 on Monday and Tuesday and chemistry lab on Wednesday, Thursday and Friday.

AUDREY: What about homework? Do you have to do a lot of homework?

ROB: Yes! All those lab reports! I have to write a report every day.

AUDREY: Oh dear. Rob?

ROB: What?

AUDREY: I have some bad news. It's one o'clock.

ROB: Oh no! I'm late for chemistry lab. I have to go.

AUDREY: Bye!

Track 45

THOMAS: Hello, I'm Thomas Harvey.

THOMAS: Pleased to meet you too. Please sit down. Now, what computer programmes can you use?

THOMAS: All right. Can you write business letters?

THOMAS: For this job you have to talk to some people in English. How good is your English?

THOMAS: You don't have to speak another foreign language for the job but it is useful. Can you speak another language?

THOMAS: What other things can you do? Things that are important for this job, like writing reports.

THOMAS: Very well. Oh, just one more thing. Can you get up early? You must be here at 7.30.

THOMAS: Thank you for coming. Don't call us, we'll call you. Goodbye.

Track 46

YOGA TEACHER: OK, everyone – camel pose. Stand up with your arms by your side. Good – relax, don't forget to breathe. Go down onto your knees and stand on your knees with your arms by your side. Bring your arms up beside your body and start to open your chest. Don't go too fast. Good – that's very good, Miriam. Now take your left hand behind you and hold your left foot. Good. Now put your right hand behind you and hold your right foot. Like this. Good – very nice. Put your head back and open your throat. That's right. Good. Jonathan! Put your head back more and open your chest more. Good. That's right and everybody hold for five breaths. Nice.

Track 47

TIM: OK. I'm ready for your instructions! Are they easy?

TIM: A square or a rectangle? Big or small?

TIM: OK, now what?

TIM: Sorry. Can you say that again? Where do I draw the straight line? In the middle?

TIM: Oh, OK. A diagonal line then, from the top left-hand corner to the bottom right-hand corner?

TIM: Four small circles, hmm, where?

TIM: Are the circles touching the sides of the square?

TIM: OK. Is that it? Look, is this OK?

Track 48

LEO: Hello?

MAGGIE: Hi Leo!

LEO: Hello Maggie!

MAGGIE: How's it going? Do you want to come to the zoo with us today?

LEO: Hmm ... maybe. What's the weather like over there?

MAGGIE: Well, it was awful yesterday, but today it's fine. It's sunny at the moment.

LEO: Really? Yesterday it was sunny all day here, but not today! It's raining here – I don't think it's a good idea to go to the zoo.

MAGGIE: But it's fine here. It's just a little bit cloudy and a bit windy, but there's no rain at all.

LEO: Is it cold?

MAGGIE: No, not at all.

LEO: Why don't we go to the cinema instead?

MAGGIE: Are there any good films on?

LEO: I hear that *Summer Rain* is good.

MAGGIE: A film about rain? No thanks.

LEO: What about the park near your house? Let's go for a walk. I don't like zoos.

MAGGIE: All right. You win. What time?

LEO: I can be at your place in an hour.

MAGGIE: OK – see you here in an hour.

Track 49

FRED: Let's go to the National Park. It's a nice day!

FRED: It's sunny. Why don't we go swimming?

FRED: Do you want to go skating?

FRED: Hey! Do you want to come to the Museum of Technology? It's really good!

Track 50

FRED: Let's go to the National Park. It's a nice day!

FRED: It's sunny. Why don't we go swimming?

FRED: Do you want to go skating?

FRED: Hey! Do you want to come to the Museum of Technology? It's really good!

Track 51

WOMAN: OK. That sounds interesting. I like technology.

WOMAN: Skating? Yes, that's a good idea!

WOMAN: Oh yes! I love going to the cinema. What film do you want to see?

WOMAN: Oh no, not the zoo! I really don't like zoos.

Track 52

a   Christopher Columbus reached America on the 12th of October 1492.

b   Did you know? The first colour television programme in the USA was in 1951!

c   Alexander Graham Bell built the first telephone in the 19th century, in 1876.

d   Mobile phones are quite new. Dr Martin Cooper invented the first one on the third of April 1973.

Track 53

INTERVIEWER: What was the most important historical moment in your lifetime?

MAN: For me, one thing that was really incredible was when Man landed on the Moon.

INTERVIEWER: Can you remember that day?

MAN: Of course! You can't forget something like that. It was 1969. I was 15.

INTERVIEWER: What happened?

MAN: Well, on 16th of July, three astronauts went into space. First they travelled in a small spacecraft, the Apollo 11. Then, on the 20th of July, two astronauts landed on the Moon in the Lunar Module. They came out and walked, actually walked, on the Moon.

INTERVIEWER: That sounds exciting!

MAN: It was very exciting. We watched the landing on television. We saw first Armstrong, then Aldrin step on the Moon. It's true what Armstrong said: 'One small step for a man; one giant leap for mankind'.

Track 54

LISA: Who is Bonita Banana?

LISA: Where was she from?

LISA: What happened to Bonita?

LISA: Why did he put her in a box?

LISA: All the way to England! What happened next?

LISA: And what happened after that?

LISA: Poor Bonita Banana!

Track 55

1   Thank you for phoning the British Museum. The museum opens Monday to Saturday from 10.00 to 5.00 and 12 noon to 6.00 on Sundays. Admission is free. The special exhibition is China Yesterday and Today. Admission to the exhibition is £8 for adults, £3 for children. The nearest tube station is Tottenham Court Road.

2   This is the Transport Museum. Opening hours are 10.00 to 6.00 daily, except Fridays when we open at 11.00. Admission is £6 for adults. Admission for children is free. Special events this month include a bus ride on the old Routemaster bus. Admission is £8 for adults. Children go free. The nearest tube station is Covent Garden.

3   Thank you for phoning the Royal Botanic Gardens at Kew. Kew Gardens open from 9.30 till dusk, eight o'clock in the summer, four o'clock in the winter. A special exhibition of tropical flowers opens from April the 16th till May the 12th. Admission is £10 for adults, £6 for children. The nearest underground station is Kew Gardens.

Track 56

BRUCE: Where did you go for your holiday?

BRUCE: Really? I'm from Australia! Where did you go?

BRUCE: I love Sydney. What do you think of the Opera House?

BRUCE: Did you go to Bondi Beach?

BRUCE: What about the Harbour Bridge? They have fantastic fireworks on New Year's Eve. Did you see that?

BRUCE: Where else did you go?

BRUCE: Really? I don't know that place. What did you do there?

BRUCE: Did you like it?

BRUCE: What was the best thing in Australia?

Track 57

CHLOE: Phew! University is finished. Now what?

PETER: Now we take a long, long holiday. I'm going to get an easy job for a few months and then I'm going to travel and see the world.

CHLOE: Don't you want to get a good job?

PETER: No, that can wait.

CHLOE: Hmm. I don't think so. I'm going to write to lots of companies and I'm going to work very hard. I'm going to earn a lot of money. And then I'm going to travel. On holiday, you know.

PETER: Great plans! Meet me on Copacabana beach. You can buy your poor friend a drink!

CHLOE: OK, it's a deal. See you in Copacabana!

Track 58

ROBERTA: I'd really like to hear about your plans!

NED: Yes, tell us about your plans. Where are you going to have the party?

ROBERTA: How lovely! But how much is that going to cost?

NED: That's OK, I guess. What about music?

NED: Isn't that going to be expensive?

ROBERTA: That sounds great! Is there going to be any food?

ROBERTA: I'm not too sure about that. Are people going to sit down at tables?

NED: What are people going to drink?

ROBERTA: Well, everything sounds just fine. But what's going to make this party special? And how much are we going to spend in total?

NED: Oh, I'm sure it's going to be a fantastic party. Thank you for all your work!

Track 59

a WOMAN: Good morning! How are you feeling after the party?

b WOMAN: Was it a good party?

c WOMAN: How was the music?

d WOMAN: What about the food? What food did you serve?

e WOMAN: Well, that sounds like a great party. Listen, do you want to organise my birthday party for me?

Track 60

a

PRESENTER: Sit back, listen and be scared! Be very scared!

NARRATOR: It was a dark winter night. The wind was blowing. It was raining hard.

WOMAN: Where am I? I can't see with all the rain. I think I'm lost!

GHOST: I know who you are. I know what you did. You can't escape.

WOMAN: Aaaargh!

b

PRESENTER: Next, the last episode of *Whodunit*? Detective Mallow talks to Dan Quite.

MALLOW: Good evening Mr Quite. I'm detective Mallow. When was the last time you saw Teresa Franco?

QUITE: Why? Where is she? What happened to Teresa?

MALLOW: That's what I want to know.

QUITE: I didn't do it! It wasn't me, I didn't kill Teresa!

MALLOW: How do you know someone killed her? I'm going to ask you to come to the police station with us. You're under arrest.

c

PRESENTER: It's time for *The Big Mistake*, a comedy for all the family.

MAN: Darling! You are the sunshine of my life! I love you! Marry me!

WOMAN: No, darling. I am not the woman you think I am.

MAN: Oh, you're right. You're not the woman I thought you were. Sorry, my mistake! I thought you were my girlfriend Lisa.

CD 2
Track 61

ANNOUNCER: ... and now here is our afternoon play, *Love is Blind*.

KATE: Well, Lorna, isn't it exciting about Kim? You are going to her party of course?

LORNA: What's exciting, Kate? What party?

KATE: You don't know about it? But Lorna ... Kim and you are best friends!

LORNA: Yes, we are best friends and I want to see her ... but she's always making excuses. I just don't understand what happened.

KATE: Well, she is getting married so she's having an engagement party. I can't believe you don't know!

LORNA: Really? Wow, that is big news. Who is she going to marry?

KATE: I don't know. It's a surprise. She's going to tell us at the party. Anyway. How are you feeling after Max?

LORNA: Well I'm very sad of course. I loved him but he doesn't love me so ...

LORNA: That's my phone. Excuse me a minute, Kate ... Hello ... Yes ... Yes, of course ... OK, no problem ... Bye ...
That was Max! He wants to see me next week. He says it's important.

Track 62

KIM: Well, Max, did you speak to Lorna?

MAX: Well, I rang her …

KIM: Yes, but when are you going to tell her?

MAX: Next week, Kim. I promise. It's difficult, you know.

KIM: Oh Max! You must tell her soon. We're getting engaged next month!

MAX: I know, I know. Next week, I promise. And now my lovely …

Track 63

a Do you feel sorry for me?

b What are you trying to say to me?

c You are not going to like this: I'm getting married.

d So you're not going out with Alex anymore?

e Oh how can you do this to me? I feel so sad!

f You broke my Blackberry™? That's so stupid! Aaargh!

Track 64

MAX: I don't know how to say this, Lorna, but … I'm getting married.

LORNA: Married? But … when? Who? It's Kim, isn't it? You're going to marry my best friend!

MAX: I'm so sorry, Lorna. Please don't be angry. Let's be friends.

LORNA: Angry? No, Max, I'm not angry. I'm sorry, sorry for Kim.

Track 65

ANNOUNCER: It's six o'clock, time for *Guess the Price!* And here is Danny!

DANNY: Welcome to the show and what a show! Our contestants tonight are Carla and Bill. For our viewers at home here are the rules. You guess the price of different items. There are two items in each round. The person who comes closer to the right price wins the round. The winner then has a chance to win great prizes. Carla, Bill, are you ready to play?

CARLA: Yes, Danny.

BILL: We are, Danny.

DANNY: Let's Guess the Price! Here we have a collection of Beatles songs on records. And we have the same Beatles collection on CDs. Which is more expensive, the records or the CDs? Guess the Price!

CARLA: I think the records are more expensive. They're difficult to find. They are £100. And the CDs are £68.

DANNY: Bill?

BILL: I think the CDs are £85 and the records are £60.

DANNY: Interesting. We'll see. Next we have a Spanish guitar and an electric guitar. Which is more expensive?

CARLA: The electric guitar is £350 and the Spanish guitar is cheaper, hmm, £150.

BILL: The Spanish guitar is £99.99 and the electric guitar is £400.

DANNY: Next round, these two beautiful sofas. Look carefully …

Track 66

DANNY: Let's reveal the prices. The Beatles records are £110, the CDs £54. The Spanish guitar is £150, the electric guitar is £370. And finally, the sofas. This sofa here is really 19th century, real leather. It's £1,358. The other one is plastic. Yours for £200. And the winner today is Carla!

Now you have the chance to win … a Mini. Oh, yes. Guess the price and you can drive home in this Mini Cooper. Are you ready?

CARLA: Is it … £10,000? How about £18,000? OK, £15,000.

DANNY: And the price is … exactly £15,260. You win! Congratulations! …

Track 67

1

MAN: Hello. I am interested in the DVD recorder you're selling. How old is it?

MAN: Oh, OK. Is it under guarantee?

MAN: Great! When can I come and see it?

2

WOMAN: Hi. I saw your ad in the paper. I'm interested in your kitchen table. How many chairs have you got?

WOMAN: It says here it's painted wood. What colour are the tables and chairs?

WOMAN: How much do you want for them?

WOMAN: Thanks. I'll think about it.

3

MAN: Hi! I'm phoning about the fridge. What brand is it?

MAN: I see. What colour is it?

MAN: Hmm. How much are you asking for it?

MAN: I can't pay that much. Can you take a little less? What's your best price?

MAN: Fair enough. When can I see the fridge? Oh and where can I see it? What's your address?

MAN: Great! See you then.

Track 68

WOMAN: Hi! I wanted to ask you about the things you wanted to sell. Did you sell everything?

WOMAN: You didn't sell the DVD recorder. Oh good! How much do you want for it?

WOMAN: Wow! That's a lot! Can you give me a special price?

WOMAN: Thank you. That's nice of you. How old is the recorder?

WOMAN: That's great! Can I give you a cheque?

WOMAN: OK. I can come and collect it tomorrow. See you then!

Track 69

CHRISTINA: Wow, Mum! Is that your new DVD recorder? It's great!

MOTHER: Yes, but I can't use the remote. There are all these buttons!

CHRISTINA: Let me see. OK, to turn it on, press this button here at the top. The one on the right.

MOTHER: I did that but nothing shows on the screen.

CHRISTINA: Ah, I know. You see this switch in the middle here? That's to decide if you want television or DVD.

MOTHER: Hey, it worked! What's this button here then? This one, look, at the top on the left.

CHRISTINA: That's the open and close button, you know, to put in a DVD.

MOTHER: OK. Now, how do I change channels?

CHRISTINA: You use the number buttons. Just press the number you want to watch.

MOTHER: That's great! But there is another problem. There is no record button! How can I record programmes?

CHRISTINA: I'm sure there is one ... Here, look, the bottom of the remote opens, like this. And here's the record button.

MOTHER: Thanks, Christina! You're so clever!

CHRISTINA: Mum, I just read the instructions.

Track 70

WOMAN: Congratulations! You are the English Learner of the Year! Tell me, what was your best experience as a learner of English this year?

WOMAN: That's great. Any embarrassing experiences? What was your most embarrassing experience as a learner of English?

WOMAN: Well, that's not so bad! Now, what's your favourite time of day to study English?

WOMAN: Why are you using a Listening and Speaking book at the moment?

WOMAN: I see. What is the best piece of technology to help you learn English more easily?

WOMAN: What are your plans and ambitions as a learner?

WOMAN: Thank you for your time. And congratulations again!

Track 71

1 a
2 u
3 e
4 o
5 i

Track 72

U, W, X, A, P, T, Y, Z, C, O, D, V, E, F, I, J, K, L, Q, R, G, H, S, M, N, B

Track 73

A, B, C, D, E, F, G, H, I, J, K, L, M, N, O, P, Q, R, S, T, U, V, W, X, Y, Z

Track 74

a Are you a doctor?
b I'm an accountant.
c He isn't an engineer.
d Marie's a student.
e Is she an architect?

Track 75

this, that, daughter, these, those, father, brother, mother, Freddy, with, bad, read

Track 76

1 sleeps, sleeps
2 works, works
3 meets, meets
4 goes, goes
5 does, does
6 plays, plays
7 flies, flies
8 watches, watches
9 washes, washes
10 relaxes, relaxes

Track 77

a foot
b tooth
c throat
d three
e healthy
f two
g month

Track 78

think, drink, thanks, having, falling, driving, watching, song, singing, going

Track 79

a Thanks for singing that song.
b I'm watching him and I think he's falling!

Track 80

a MAN 1: Oh good. You're here.
   MAN 2: Yes, we're here but they're there.
b MAN 1: Is everybody ready?
   MAN 2: I'm ready. He's ready and she's ready. But now it's raining!

Track 81

love, money, does, lot, on

Track 82

club, Hong Kong, but, London, wrong, touch, stop, doesn't, contact

Track 83

bedrooms, boxes, desks, eyes, lamps, sisters, sofas, tables

Track 84

a Is there a bank near here?
b Are there any shops near here?
c There is a post office near the supermarket.

Track 85

a MAN: Is there a hospital in this town?
   WOMAN: Yes, there is. It's near the car park.
b WOMAN: Are there any supermarkets near here?
   MAN: Yes, there are. There are two.
c MAN: Where is the town hall?
   WOMAN: There isn't a town hall here.

Track 86
a Can you play the piano?
b No, I can't.
c Yes, I can.

Track 87
MARIA: Can you speak French?
JAMIE: No, I can't. I can speak Dutch and German, but I can't speak French. Can you?
MARIA: Yes, I can.

Track 88
a mouse
b rhino

Track 89
a Look out for the mouse.
b That's too loud now. Turn it down.
c Mind the wild animal.
d Find the white dog.
e There's a mouse in the house.
f Put your right hand behind you.

Track 90
d d d, died
t t t, finished
id id id, landed
died, died
ended, ended
finished, finished
jumped, jumped
kissed, kissed
landed, landed
lifted, lifted
lived, lived
played, played
studied, studied
wanted, wanted
watched, watched
worked, worked

Track 91
a played, turned, lived, liked. Liked is different, liked.
b kissed, cooked, died, watched. Died is different, died.
c wanted, beheaded, washed, decided. Washed is different, washed.
d arrived, reached, loved, divorced. Reached is different, reached.
e landed, ended, lifted, happened. Happened is different, happened.
f started, worked, baked, walked. Started is different, started.

Track 92
later, letter; later, letter
late, let; late, let
tale, tell; tale, tell
paper, pepper; paper, pepper
wait, wet; wait, wet

Track 93
a will, wheel; will, wheel
b eat, it; eat, it
c least, list; least, list
d Tim, team; Tim, team
e feel, fill; feel, fill

Track 94
a Sit down and eat your meat.
b Please take a seat, Phil.
c Tim's team is going to win.
d Listen and fill in the blanks on your sheet.
e This machine's very quick.

Track 95
a Are you going to ask her to come?
b I'm going to tell you a secret.
c How's it going to end?
d They're going to have a party.

Track 96
a I'm going to ask you a question and you're going to answer.
b You're going to talk and I'm going to listen.
c I'm going to open the door. Are you going to come in?

Track 97
burn, world, turn, bird, girl

Track 98
ten, tan, tonne, turn
pan, pen, pun
Dad, dead
cat, cut
Kurt, cup
cap

Track 99
a I plan to marry Jerry.
b I heard it had two heads!
c Ben burnt the buns.

Track 100
a Brazil – Brazilian
b Canada – Canadian
c Russia – Russian
d Japan – Japanese
e China – Chinese
f Korea – Korean
g Mexico – Mexican
h Australia – Australian
i South Africa – South African

Track 101
a How much is this dress?
b How much are those shoes?
c How much does it cost?
d How much are the apples?
e How much is that cheese?
f How many do you want?

Track 102

a How many apples do you want?
b How much bread do you want?
c How many eggs do you want?
d How much salad do you want?
e How much does this meat cost?
f How many bananas do you want?

Track 103

a How much is that shirt?
b Can you speak slowly, please?
c She's got dark brown hair.
d He's got light blue eyes.
e Can I take a message?
f How much does it cost?

Track 104

a I don't have to go.
b I have to go.

Track 105

a We have to prepare for the test.
b They don't have to get up early.
c She has to send emails.
d He doesn't have to speak French at work.

Track 106

a I have to wait in the gym.
   I have two weights in the gym.
b They don't have two plays in the theatre.
   They don't have to play in the theatre.
c She has two works in the museum.
   She has to work in the museum.

Track 107

a Sue's taller than John.
b John's older than Sue.
c This book's shorter than that one.
d She's nicer than he is.

Track 108

a Beaches are hotter than mountains.
b This book's more interesting than that one.
c Bob's shorter than Peter.
d He's more attractive than Peter.
e Miranda's as clever as Tim.
f Today's better than yesterday and not as good as tomorrow.

Track 109

a Are you married?
b Are you a teacher?
c Are you English?
d Do you like chocolate?
e Does your friend eat snacks?

Track 110

a What's your name?
   Where do you live?
b Do you like playing football?
   Does he live in France?
c When does she go shopping?
   Does she go shopping on Fridays?
d Do they like travelling?
   When do they travel?

Track 111

a What's your name?
b Do you live here?
c Where do you live?
d When do you go shopping?
e Do you like travelling?
f Does he work in a bank?

Track 112

a That's awful!
   That's great!
b I hate shopping.
   I love shopping.
c I'm very tired.
   I'm very happy.
d It's too cold.
   It's too hot.

Track 113

a (That's terrible!)
b (That's great!)
c (I love hot weather!)
d (I hate cold weather!)
e (It was awful!)
f (It was lovely!)

Track 114

a That's terrible!
b That's great!
c I love hot weather!
d I hate cold weather!
e It was awful!
f It was lovely!

Answer key

Unit 1

A Listening

2 a Conversation 3
   b Conversation 2
   c Conversation 1
   d Conversation 4

3 a Frank
   b Frank
   c Cecilia
   d Claudio, Paula

B Speaking

1 a Hi
   b My name's
   c This is
   d Nice to meet you.
   e How are you?

2 a My name's (Alex)
   b Pleased to meet you

4 My name's (Chris).
   Nice to meet you too.
   Hi, Marco. Pleased to meet you.
   Not bad, thank you.

Unit 2

A Listening

1 All phrases should be ticked.

2 a 5 b 1 c 2

3 Hi. *Inf*
   Hello. *either*
   Good morning. *either*
   Good afternoon. *F*
   Good evening. *F*
   How are you ? *either*
   How's it going? *Inf*
   I'm very well, thank you. *F*
   Fine, thanks. *Inf*
   Very well, thanks. *Inf*
   Fine, thank you. *either*
   Not bad, thanks. *Inf*
   And you? *either*
   You? *Inf*

B Speaking

1 a Hi, Caroline. How are you?
   b – Good afternoon.
      – How are you?
   c – Good evening,
      – Hello
      – Very well, thanks.
   d – Hi Lucy! How's it going?
      – Fine, thanks.

3 Hi. I'm (Alex)
   Are you
   Are you

Unit 3

A Listening

1 sixteen, seventeen, nineteen

3 a 0208 495 3497
   b 0703 034856
   c 0178 82545
   d 07882 945 620

4 a at, dot
   b underscore, at, dot, dot

B Speaking

1 a Maria
   b Lozano
   c Spanish
   d mariloz@yahoo.com
   e 0207 857 2496

2 a What's your name?
   b Where are you from?
   c And your phone number?

3 Hello, the Just Right School of English!
   Sure. What's your name?
   How do you spell your last name?
   Thanks. Where are you from, Claire?
   What's your email address?
   Great. And your phone number?
   Thanks. I'll send you the information immediately.

Unit 4

A Listening

1 Zack Jones: fair skin, short straight blonde hair, blue eyes
   Olivia Stott: fair skin, long straight brown hair, green eyes
   Miriam Okyere: dark skin, curly black hair, black eyes
   Joseph Smith: dark skin, short curly grey hair, brown eyes
   Susan Lee: olive skin, long straight black hair, brown eyes
   Kenny Williams: fair skin, short straight red hair, green eyes

3 a The baby in picture a is Susan Lee.
   b The baby in picture b is Zack Jones.
   c The baby in picture c is Miriam Okyere.
   d The baby in picture d is Kenny Williams.
   e The baby in picture e is Olivia Stott.
   f The baby in picture f is Joseph Smith.

4 picture a – Susan Lee
   picture c – Joseph Smith
   picture f – Miriam Okyere
   picture d – Zack Jones
   picture e – Olivia Stott
   picture b – Kenny Williams

5 Number of names the friends guessed: 2

B Speaking

3 *Sample answer:*
   My name's Tom.
   I'm from Belgium. And you?
   I have short hair.
   No, my hair is blonde.
   My eyes are blue.
   OK. Bye !

Unit 5

A Listening

1 a B
   b A
   c A
   d A
   e B
   f B
   g A and B

2 1 Clapham Junction
   2 Southampton
   3 Miami
   4 Rio de Janeiro
   5 Mexico City

3 1 Time: 7.15, Platform 2
   2 Time: 7.25, Platform 6
   3 Flight number: 308, Gate 13A
   4 Flight number: 407, Gate 30A
   5 Flight number 601, Gate 10
   Julian Jones: 3

B Speaking
2 I really like – I love
  I really don't like – I hate
3 *Sample answer:*
  No, I hate Mondays too.
  I work and I watch television.
  My favourite day is Friday.
  I meet my friends and I go to the
  cinema. What about you?

Unit 6
A Listening
1 a cheese
  b tea
  c milk
  d vegetables
  e bread
  f hamburgers
  g chicken
  h fruit
  i orange juice
  j cake
  k ice cream
2 Ad 3
3 f hamburgers; £2.50
  g chicken; £4.80
  h oranges; 50p
  j chocolate cake; £3.50

B Speaking
2 a Do you eat snacks?
  b Do you eat fish twice a week?
  c Do you drink eight glasses of
    water every day?
  d Do you eat hamburgers every
    day?
  e Do you often have ice cream?
  f Do you drink three cups of
    coffee or tea every day?
3 Can I ask you some questions for a
  questionnaire?
  Do you eat snacks?
  Do you eat hamburgers every day?
  Do you drink eight glasses of water
  every day?
  Do you eat fish twice a week?
  Do you drink three cups of coffee
  or tea every day?
  Do you have ice cream often?

Unit 7
A Listening
1 a action film
  b horror film
  c comedy
  d romantic film

2 *Small Adventures*: c (comedy)
  Terror in London: b (horror film)
  Always: d (romantic film)
  Today's Hero: a (action film)
3 a One b family c 3 p.m., 5 p.m.
  d One e 18 f 9.30 p.m.
  g Two h *Always* i all
  j 7.15 p.m, 9.45 p.m.
  k Three l *Today's Hero* m film
  n 3.30 p.m., 8.30 p.m.

B Speaking
1 a S
  b S
  c S
  d D
  e D
2 Where do you live?
  Do you live in Hollywood?
  Do you like the cinema?
  What is your favourite film?
  Do you have a hobby?
  Do you work in a cinema?
  Are you Rowena Robertson?

Unit 8
A Listening
1 a head
  b leg, arm
  c stomach, hand
  d leg, foot
2 a 2
  c 3
  d 1
3 a 5
  b His leg hurts.
  c Michael James
  d His head hurts.
  e Melanie
  f 3
4 a right there
  b Take care
  b What's the matter?
  c Let me see.

B Speaking
1 a I'll be right there.
  b Let me see. What's the matter?
  c Let me see.
3 *Sample answer:*
  My head often hurts.
  Yes, I sometimes have a lot of
  work.
  Yes, I use a computer at work.
  I don't exercise often.
  I occasionally eat a good breakfast.
  I sometimes watch television.

Unit 9
A Listening
2 jeans, shorts, trainers, a skirt
3 black dress, green dress, T-shirts,
  sandals, casual shirt, grey suits
4 a dresses
  b green
  c 4.99
  d L
  e 49.99
  f grey
  g sandals
  h shirts
  i M
  j L

B Speaking
3 *Sample answer:*
  I want to buy an MP3 player.
  OK. Let's buy five CDs.
  I want to buy just drinks: milk,
  coffee and tea.
  Yes, but I also want to buy a warm
  jacket and some boots.
  That's £154.00
  That's a good idea!

Unit 10
A Listening
1 1 d The people are wearing
      uniforms.
  2 c The people are watching and
      clapping.
  3 b The child is dancing.
  4 a The band is playing.
2 2, 3, 4
  The speakers do not talk about
  picture 1.
3 a beautiful day
  b it is, sun
  c band, clothes, yellow, red,
    green, black
  d listen, music
  e is playing
4 a in a stadium
  b athletes
  c sports clothes, uniforms
  d they are waving
  e it is at night

B Speaking
1 a Tom
  b Tina and Katie
  c Mia
  d Alex
  e Nicky
  f Anna

g Sam
h Jill and Andy
3 Yes I have.
Yes, he is.
No, he's riding a bike.
He's dancing.
No, Anna's listening to Nicky. He's playing the guitar.
He's climbing a tree.
Yes, I have.
Tina and Katie are playing baseball.
Mia's walking.
Jill's dancing and Anna's listening to Nicky.
We have four differences.

Unit 11
A Listening
1 **clothes:** suit, T-shirt, dress, shoes, jacket, shirt, tie, trousers, sweater
adjectives: green, brown, great, pink, white, black, nice, original, short, elegant
2 a 2
b 1
c 4
d 3
4 dress – great winter clothes for young women
suit – great colour
casual trousers and sweater – nice but not very original; great for men of all ages
suit – very elegant

B Speaking
1 Don is short. He has brown hair. He's wearing black trousers, a denim jacket and a red shirt.
Daniel is tall and slim. He has red hair. He's wearing a pink suit, a yellow shirt and a brown tie. He's handsome.
Monica is slim. She has brown hair. She's wearing a black dress and black boots. She's carrying a white jumper. She's elegant.
Richard is tall and slim. He has red hair. He's wearing a brown suit, a pink shirt and a yellow tie. He looks fashionable.
2 a How tall is she?
b What is she wearing?
c What does she look like?
d What's his/her hair like?

3 *Sample answer:*
The person's not very tall.
The person's slim and has long hair.
The person's wearing a dress and boots.
Yes, it is.
How tall is the person?
What does the person look like?
Is it a man or a woman?
Is the person wearing a suit?
Is it Richard?

Unit 12
A Listening
1 a letter
b phone call
c email
d fax
2 a T
b DK
c F
d T
e T
f T
3 a Cath
b Tim
c Cath
d Tim
e Cath
4 1 Tim's sending a **fax** for **Mr Roberts.**
2 meeting with **the manager** at **3.00**
3 meet **Tim** at 8 o'clock at **the restaurant**
5 1 Tim's sending a **fax** for **the manager.**
2 meeting with **Mr Roberts** at **4.00**
3 meet **Frank** for **dinner** at **8 o'clock**
Cath's four mistakes:
a The fax is for Mr Roberts, not for the manager.
b The meeting is with the manager, not with Mr Roberts.
c The meeting is at 3 o'clock, not 4 o'clock.
d Dinner is with Tim, not with Frank.

B Speaking
2 *Sample answer:*
Sure.
Yes, I often use a computer.

I often use the Internet.
I use it for work and I send emails to friends and family.
Yes, I sometimes write cards and letters.
I use my mobile for important things.
No, I don't have a web page.
Because I don't need one.
You're welcome.

Unit 13
A Listening
1 a on
b in
c under
d opposite
e next to
f between
g near
2 a watch
b mobile phone
c sweater
d sweatshirt
e dog
f child
g handbag
h wallet
3 1 mobile phone
2 sweater
3 child
4 dog
5 wallet
4 a 1
d 2
f 3
h 4
i 5

B Speaking
2 I've got a big sofa next to the window.
I've got a small sofa opposite the big sofa.
I've got a big lamp next to the big sofa.
I've got a small table between the sofas.
I've got a small lamp on the small table.
I've got a rug under the table.
I've got a bookcase near the window.
3 a Yes, I have. I've got two sofas.
b The big one is yellow and the small one is brown.
c No, I haven't got any chairs.

d Yes, I've got a coffee table.

e My coffee table is between the sofas.

f Yes, I am very happy with my new room.

g My favourite thing is the big sofa.

5 It's beautiful.

Oh, yes. I've got two sofas, one big and one small. I've also got a small table and two lamps.

The big sofa is next to the window.

The small sofa is opposite the big sofa.

The small table is between the two sofas.

The big lamp is next to the big sofa and the small lamp is on the table.

Yes, I've got one red rug.

I haven't got a television.

Unit 14

A Listening

1 a swimming pool

b terrace

c balcony

d tennis court

e garden

2 picture 1

3 a F

b T

c F

d F

e T

f F

g T

B Speaking

1 a cinema

b theatre

c restaurant

d shopping centre

e supermarket

f school

g hospital

h park

4 *Sample answer:*

I live in Nantes.

It's great.

There are many shops, shopping centres and supermarkets.

There are cinemas and theatres.

Yes, because there are good schools and nice parks.

Yes, there is a large hospital. How about you? What's your town like?

Is there a shopping centre?

Is it a good place to live?

Unit 15

A Listening

1 1 e 2 a 3 f 4 c 5 b 6 d

2 a the news

b sports programme

c the weather forecast

d play

3 a T

b F

c F

d T

e F

f F

4 a music programme

5 Susie, Kevin and Jack, Joanne and Brian

6 a April 3rd

b April 4th

c April 2nd

7 a listening to, 95.4

b two, love

c show, song, sons

d wife, fourth birthday, anniversary, birthday

B Speaking

3 *Sample answer:*

Hi. My name's Marie.

I'm calling from Brighton.

I'd like to hear *Where are we going?* by Ilene Barnes.

Yes, it's for my friend Julie.

She is moving to a new home.

Happy new home, Julie.

Yes, please. I'd like to hear *Lead me, Father* by Johnny Cash.

It's for my Dad.

Happy birthday, Dad!

Unit 16

A Listening

3 chemistry, biology

Rob studies science, maybe microbiology.

4 No, Rob doesn't like his timetable, because he has a lot of work. He has a class every day at 9 a.m. and he hates getting up early. He has to be in the lab every day till 5 o'clock.

5

	9.00–11.00	1.00–5.00
M	biology	biology lab
T	chemistry	biology lab
W	biology	chemistry lab
Th	chemistry	chemistry lab
F	biology	chemistry lab

B Speaking

3 Hello, pleased to meet you.

I can use Word, Excel, PowerPoint and Outlook.

Yes, of course, I can write business letters.

I think my English is good.

Yes, I can speak Spanish too.

I can write reports and do presentations too.

That's fine. I like getting up early. Goodbye.

Unit 17

A Listening

1

head, back, arm, stomach, throat, chest, leg, foot, knee

2 1 c 2 d 3 b 4 a 5 e

3 a camel

b back, leg, stomach

c feet

4 c, a, b, e, d

5 a arms

b forget

c knees

d open

e Don't

f hold

g hand

h head

6 good, that's very good, very nice, that's right, nice

B Speaking

1 a rectangle

b corner

c circle

d triangle

e straight line

f square

2 a There's a blue dot at the top of the triangle.

b There's a pink dot in the bottom left-hand corner of the rectangle.

c There's a red dot in the middle of the circle.

d There's a black dot in the top right-hand corner of the square.

e There's a green dot at the bottom of the straight line.

3 Draw a square. Draw a straight line from the top left-hand corner to the bottom right-hand corner of the square. Put four small circles on each side of the square, one at the top, one at the bottom, one on the left, one on the right.

4 You'll see! Draw a shape.
A big square.
Now put a straight line in the square.
The line goes from the top left-hand corner to the bottom right-hand corner.
That's right. Now, draw four small circles.
One on each side of the square.
Yes, they are.
That's very good.

Unit 18
A Listening
1 a raining
b cloudy
c sunny
d windy
e snowing
3 a windy
b raining
c sunny, a little cloudy, windy
4 picture c
5 a T
b T
c F
d F
e T
f F
6 a today
b yesterday
c today
d fine, cloudy, windy, rain
e films
f *Summer Rain*
g walk, zoos
h hour

B Speaking
3 *Sample answer:*
a Let's go to the Museum of Technology.
b Why don't we go skating?
c Do you want to go to the cinema?
d Let's go to the zoo.
4 Your friend likes the first three ideas, but not the zoo.

Unit 19
A Listening
1 a 12 October 1492
b 1951
c 1876
d 3 April 1973
4 Picture a
5 a T
b F
c T
d F
e F
f T
6 a

B Speaking
1 a Central America
b banana
c farmer
d box
e fly
f supermarket shelf
g skin
h bin
2 This is the story of Bonita Banana. Bonita grew up in Central America. First a farmer picked her. Then he packed her in a box. Next she flew to England on a plane. After that, someone put her on a supermarket shelf. A woman bought her. Finally, a little boy ate her and put the skin in a bin.
3 Listen. I'm going to tell you the story of Bonita Banana.
Bonita Banana was a banana.
She was from Central America.
First a farmer picked her. Then he packed her in a box.
He put her in a box to fly to England.
Next someone put her on a supermarket shelf.
A woman bought her and a little boy ate her and put the skin in a bin.

Unit 20
A Listening
1 a, b, c, e, h
2 a 1 Kew Gardens
2 Covent Garden
3 Tottenham Court Road
b Opening hours
c Special Events
d Admission
3 The British Museum b
The Transport Museum c
The Royal Botanic Gardens a
4 a Opening hours: 9.30 – 4.00 (winter) / 8.00 (summer)
Admission: £10 adults, £6 children
b Opening hours: 10.00 – 5.00 (12.00 – 6.00 Sundays)
Admission: free (exhibition: £8 adults, £3 children)
c Opening hours: 10.00 – 6.00 (Fridays 11.00 – 6.00)
Admission: £6 adults, free for children (special event: £8 adults, free for children)
5 a The Royal Botanic Gardens
b The Transport Museum
c The British Museum

B Speaking
1 a Bondi Beach
b Great Barrier Reef
c Opera House
d Great Barrier Reef, Bondi Beach
e Blue Mountains National Park, Ayers Rock
f Harbour Bridge
Around Sydney: a, c, d, e, f
3 *Sample answer:*
I went to Australia.
I went to Sydney.
It's great.
Yes, I went surfing there.
Yes, it was fantastic.
I also went to the Great Barrier Reef.
I went snorkelling.
I loved it.
The Great Barrier Reef was the best thing for me.

Unit 21
A Listening
1 a They graduated from university.
b happy, excited
c *students' own answer*

2 a They graduated from university:
P + C

b happy, excited: P + C

c get a job: P + C;
see the world: P

3 a Peter

b Peter

c Chloe

d Peter

e Chloe

f Chloe

4 Peter: can

Chloe: don't think, lots of, going
to, a lot of

Peter: Great, can

Chloe says: 'OK, it's a deal. See
you in Copacabana.'

B Speaking

2 *Sample answer:*

I'm going to have the party in the
University garden.

It's going to cost £100.

I'm going to ask *The Tropical
Nuts*. It's a good band.

No, it's only £100.

Yes, of course. It's going to be a
hot dinner.

Oh, yes. I'm going to spend £100
on chic tables.

I'm going to have soft drinks and
wine, but not expensive wine.

I think the band is going to make
the party special. We're going to
spend about £1000.

4 *Sample answer:*

a Fine but very tired.

b It was a fantastic party.

c The band was great.

d We served hot dinners. The food
was delicious.

e OK. Have you got £1000? ...

Unit 22

A Listening

1 A horror story

B thriller

C comedy

2 A scared, dark, escape

B Whodunit, detective, kill, police

C mistake, comedy, family

3 The play's going to be romantic
and dramatic.

4 a T

b F

c T

d F

e F

f F

5 e

6 a speak

b rang

c tell

d week

e difficult

f engaged

g month

7 Different. Corrected summary:
6.15 *Love is Blind*. Max <u>hasn't
told</u> Lorna that he is getting
married. Kim <u>wants Lorna to
know very soon</u>. Max talks to
Lorna <u>next week</u>.

B Speaking

1 a 2 **b** 5 **c** 1 **d** 6 **e** 3 **f** 4

a I feel sorry for Caroline.

b I don't know how to say this
but I'm going to get married.

c You're going to marry my best
friend, aren't you?

d No but I hope we can be
friends.

e I'm sorry I made you sad.

f Please don't get angry.

Unit 23

A Listening

1 1 c **2** b **3** f **4** a **5** d **6** e

2 a F

b T

c F

d T

e T

4 Beatles collection: records £110,
CDs £54

Guitars: Spanish £150, electric
£370

Sofas: leather £1,358, plastic £200

Car: £15,260

B Speaking

1 a the fridge

b the kitchen table with chairs

c the DVD recorder

d the flat screen television

2 *Sample answer:*

Phone call 1

How old is it?

It is brand new.

Oh, OK. Is it under guarantee?

Yes, it is.

Can you come this afternoon?

Phone call 2

How many chairs have you got?

I have got four chairs.

It says here it's painted wood.

What colour are the tables and
chairs?

They are white.

How much do you want for them?

£100.

Phone call 3

What brand is it?

It's a Zanussi.

I see. What colour is it?

It is white.

Hmm. How much are you asking
for it?

£300.

Hmm. *£280?*

Where can I see it? What's your
address?

100 Stamford Road.

4 *Sample answer:*

a No. I sold the TV, the fridge,
the table and chairs.

b £250? It's a Panasonic!

c OK, what about £230?

d It's brand new.

e Yes, a cheque is fine.

Unit 24

A Listening

1 *Sample answer:*

1 Why don't you read them? /
Read them again slowly and
carefully.

2 Play with the different buttons
and see what happens.

3 Calm down. / Look at the
pictures in the instructions.

4 Read the instructions slowly
and carefully again.

5 Calm down. / Ask a member of
your family to help. / Get a
simpler machine! / Pay a
technician. / Ask the people at
the shop to explain.

2 power 1

TV/DVD 2

open/close 3

numbers 4

record 5

3 a T

b F

c T

d F

e T
f F
g T
4 a recorder
  b remote
  c turn (it) on
  d top
  e screen
  f switch
  g decide

B Speaking

1/2 *students' own answer*

Pronunciation exercises

A Sounds

3

/eɪ/ A, H, J, K
/iː/ B, C, D, E, G, P, T, V
/e/ F, L, M, N, S, X, Z
/aɪ/ I, Y
/əʊ/ O
/uː/ Q, U, W
/ɑː/ R

6

/ð/ this, that, these, those, father, brother, mother, with
/d/ daughter, Freddy, bad, read

8

/s/ sleeps, works, meets
/z/ goes, plays, flies, does
/ɪz/ watches, relaxes, washes

9

/t/: foot, tooth, throat, two
/θ/: tooth, throat, three, healthy, month

15

1 You're 2 we're 3 they're
4 Is everybody 5 I'm 6 He's 7 she's

16

lot, on

17

/ʌ/ love, club, but, touch, doesn't
/ɒ/ Hong Kong, London, wrong, stop, contact

18

/s/ bedrooms, desks, lamps, tables
/z/ eyes, sisters, sofas
/ɪz/ boxes

19

a /s/
b /z/
c /ɪz/

20

a Is there a bank near here?
b Are there any shops near here?

c There is a post office near the supermarket.

21

a Is there a hospital in this town?
  Yes, there is. It's near the car park.
b Are there any supermarkets near here?
  Yes, there are. There are two.
c Where is the town hall?
  There isn't a town hall here.

22

a /ə/
b /ɑː/
c /æ/
1 /æ/
2 /ə/
3 /ɑː/

23

Maria: /ə/
Jamie: /ɑː/, /ə/, /ɑː/, /ə/
Maria: /æ/

24

a /aʊ/
b /aɪ/

25

a Look out for the mouse.
b That's too loud now. Turn it down.
c Mind the wild animal.
d Find the white dog.
e There's a mouse in the house.
f Put your right hand behind you.

26

/d/ died, played, studied
/t/ finished, jumped, kissed, lived, watched, worked
/ɪd/ ended, landed, lifted, wanted

27

a liked
b died
c washed
d reached
e happened
f started

28

/eɪ/ eight, later, late, tale, paper, wait
/e/ bed, letter, let, tell, pepper, wet

31

/iː/ meat, please, seat, sheet
/ɪ/ sit, Phil, win, listen, in, this, machine, quick

32

a /tə/ ask, /tuː/ come
b /tuː/ tell
c /tə/ end
d /tuː/ have

33

a /tə/ ask, /tə/ answer
b /tuː/ talk, /tuː/ listen
c /tə/ open, /tuː/ come

35/36

/e/ bed, Ben, ten, pen, dead, Jerry, heads
/æ/ bad, ban, tan, pan, Dad, cat, cap, plan, marry, had
/ʌ/ bud, bun, tonne, pun, cut, cup
/ɜː/ bird, burn, turn, Kurt, heard, burnt

B Stress

1

a Brazil – Brazilian
b Canada – Canadian
c Russia – Russian
d Japan – Japanese
e China – Chinese
f Korea – Korean
g Mexico – Mexican
h Australia – Australian
i South Africa – South African

3

Mexican, British, South African, Russian

Korean, Australian, Brazilian, Canadian

Canadian – Canada
Japan – Japanese
China – Chinese

4

a dress
b shoes
c cost
d apples
e cheese
f want

5

a apples
b bread
c eggs
d salad
e meat
f bananas

6

a shirt
b slowly
c dark brown
d light blue
e message
f cost

7

a have
b have

9

a wait, two

b two, play

c two, work

10

a Sue, taller, John

b John, older, Sue

c This book, shorter, that one

d She, nicer, he

Than is pronounced /ðən/.

11

a beaches, hotter, mountains

b this book, interesting, that

c Bob, shorter, Peter

d he, attractive, Peter

e Miranda, clever, Tim

f Today, better, yesterday, not, good, tomorrow

comparative adjective, *are*, *than*

more, *as*

C Intonation

1

They all go up.

3

a same

b same

c different

d different

4

a down

b up

c down

d down

e up

f up

6

a S

b H

c H

d S

e S

f H

Notes